Smart Love Solutions in Early Childhood

Also by Martha Heineman Pieper, Ph.D.
and William J. Pieper, M.D.

Smart Love
Addicted to Unhappiness

Smart Love Solutions in Early Childhood
A Handbook for Parents, Teachers, and Caregivers

Martha Heineman Pieper, Ph.D.
William J. Pieper, M.D.

Published by Smart Love Family Services

Smart Love Family Services
Smart Love Preschool
800 W. Buena Ave
Chicago, Illinois 60613
p: 773.665.8052
f: 773.525.4097
contact@smartlovefamily.org
www.smartlovefamily.org
www.smartlovepreschool.org

Smart Love Solutions in Early Childhood

ISBN: 978-0-9826790-0-5

Copyright © 2010 by Martha Heineman Pieper, Ph.D., and William J. Pieper, M.D., Published by Smart Love Family Services, 2010.

The purpose of this book is to educate. It is sold with the understanding that the author and publisher shall have neither liability nor responsibility for any injury caused or alleged to be caused directly or indirectly by the information found in this book. While every effort has been made to ensure the book's accuracy, its contents should not be construed as medical advice. Each person's needs are unique. To obtain recommendations appropriate to your particular situation, please consult a qualified professional.

The greatest improvement in the quality of human life
will come not from brilliant discoveries about the nature of
matter or technological innovations, but from parents
whose love and insight give their children lasting inner happiness
and thereby leave a legacy of competent, caring individuals.

–Martha Heineman Pieper, Ph.D., & William J. Pieper, M.D.
Smart Love

Contents

Foreward

♥

It is a pleasure to bring you this new and expanded volume of *Smart Love* solutions to common questions about how best to respond to young children. Our hope is that *Smart Love Solutions in Early Childhood* will guide parents, teachers, and caregivers both in the home and in the classroom, to nurture happy, healthy and successful children.

The *Smart Love* approach was developed by child development experts and parents of five, Martha Heineman Pieper, Ph.D., and William J. Pieper, M.D. *Smart Love* helps parents raise happy children who over time come to regulate their own behavior within a deeply satisfying parent-child relationship. Endorsed by child development experts here and abroad, *Smart Love* is a unique, evidence-informed approach to parenting and child development.

Smart Love Family Services opened its doors soon after *Smart Love* was published. Smart Love Family Services is a non-profit organization, founded to promote kind and compassionate guidance to children. We offer a range of services such as: child development classes, counseling, parent coaching, and training and consultation in the *Smart Love* approach to other agencies. We are adding Smart Love Preschool to our "family" of services. Smart Love Preschool provides a play-based curriculum for children ages 3, 4, and 5 as well as programs for infants and toddlers with their parents or caregivers. We are pleased to publish *Smart Love Solutions* to complement this important extension into preschool education.

Carolyn Stolper Friedman
Executive Director
Smart Love Family Services and Smart Love Preschool

Introduction

For years parents asked us their most pressing questions, and we responded to them in our monthly "Smart Love" column in Chicago Parent and as frequent contributors on the parenting site babycenter.com. This handbook is a compilation of the questions we have answered to guide parents, teachers and caregivers through the early years.

We are psychotherapists, consultants to other mental health professionals, and parents of five children. Our work with unhappy and difficult children, our experience with children who were thriving, and our ongoing parenting responsibilities combined to show us how vital it is for children to see themselves as loving and lovable. This work also led us to a new understanding of the goals of childhood and how to best help children attain them.

With the benefit of this large pool of experience, we developed the concepts that comprise the *Smart Love* approach. Initially, we set forth our conclusions about child development and mental illness in *Intrapsychic Humanism,* a text written expressly for professionals and academics. As word about *Intrapsychic Humanism* began to spread within the professional and academic worlds, we were repeatedly asked whether we would write a book specifically for parents. That decision was the genesis of our book, *Smart Love: The Compassionate Alternative to Discipline that Will Make You a Better Parent and Your Child a Better Person* (Harvard Common Press, 1999). We have since published a self-help book geared toward adults called, *Addicted to Unhappiness: Free Yourself From Moods and Behaviors that Undermine Relationships, Work, and the Life You Want* (McGraw Hill, 2003).

In our book, *Smart Love,* we offer practical guidelines that enable parents to give their children the specific kind of love they need to grow into happy, fulfilled adults. We've seen the effectiveness of our unique approach with children, adolescents, and parents from all walks of life and from different racial, ethnic, economic, and cultural backgrounds.

The *Smart Love* approach guides you to help your child make constructive choices in the context of an ongoing close relationship. If you use these guidelines, your child will come to recognize that the deepest happiness results from loving and feeling lovable and loved, rather than from satisfying particular desires or achieving specific goals. Your child will learn to govern her/himself better through the desire to feel happier and more competent than s/he ever would from fear of negative consequences.

Our approach teaches you how to best satisfy your child's developmental needs and how to manage her/his immature behaviors. With the guidelines we provide, you can help your child acquire a stable inner well-being that is unaffected by success, failure, or other ups and downs of daily life; and that will enable your child to reach her/his full potential.

Parents and professionals alike often ask us about other parenting approaches that advocate using discipline or permissiveness to guide their children. *Smart Love* is unique because it replaces both of those methods with what we call *loving regulation*. Loving regulation means you stop the child from doing whatever behavior you think is inappropriate at that moment, but you maintain closeness with them, and you don't impose any unpleasant consequences. The point isn't to get kids to do what you say, but to try to help them learn to make good choices. That's what loving regulation is all about. You stay positive with your child. Children learn that they may not be able to have the thing they want at a given moment, but they can always have a close relationship with you. That's why loving regulation actually produces children who are the opposite of spoiled, because material things do not assume such incredible importance to them. We have learned that if you put the time in at the crucial moments of development, then your job as parents will be easier as the child grows older because your child will become naturally happy and autonomous. Kids who are unhappy consume an enormous amount of adult time. The good news is that at any point in a child's life, even as adults, we can help them become happier people. If parents have gotten bad advice and been overly harsh with children, it's never too late to change to the *Smart Love* approach and help children become happier and more fuctional.

The *Smart Love* approach is based on the most current research about child development. It is the first parenting approach that helps you see the world through your child's eyes at each stage of development. It helps you see your children as children, which will help you relax and enjoy them. This takes the worry out of parenting. It tells people what to expect and what to do. We're offering parents a different way to parent that is much more enjoyable and will produce happier and more responsible children.

This year we are taking the *Smart Love* philosophy into the classroom and opening Smart Love Preschool in Chicago. Our hope with this new endeavor and the publication of *Smart Love Solutions in Early Childhood: A Handbook for Parents, Teachers and Caregivers* is that our children have as many enjoyable hours as possible, whether inside the classroom, at home, or out in the world.

Martha Heineman Pieper, Ph.D.
William J. Pieper, M.D.

About the Authors

Martha Heineman Pieper, Ph.D., and William J. Pieper, M.D., are co-authors of numerous articles and books, including *Intrapsychic Humanism: An Introduction to a Comprehensive Psychology and Philosophy of Mind* (Falcon II Press, 1990); *Smart Love: The Compassionate Alternative to Discipline that Will Make You a Better Parent and Your Child a Better Person* (Harvard Common Press, 1999, 2001), and *Addicted to Unhappiness: Free Yourself from Moods and Behaviors that Undermine Relationships, Work, and the Life Your Want* (McGraw-Hill, 2002, 2004). The Piepers also wrote a monthly column, *Smart Love,* for *Chicago Parent.* They have conducted numerous workshops for professionals and parents, and Martha Heineman Pieper has made appearances on Fox TV, NBC TV, and numerous talk radio shows. For over thirty years they have conducted clinical research and been in private practice treating children, adolescents, and adults; counseling parents; and supervising other mental health professionals.

Martha Heineman Pieper graduated Phi Beta Kappa and Magna Cum Laude from Radcliffe College, and received her Ph.D. in clinical social work from the University of Chicago. She has served on the editorial board of professional journals such as *Illinois Child Welfare, Social Work* and *Smith College Studies in Social Work.* In addition to her clinical writings she has published extensively on the topic of philosophy of research. She is on the Board of Directors of Smart Love Family Services and the Intrapsychic Humanism Society.

William J. Pieper received his B.S. and M.D. degrees from the University of Illinois. He completed residencies in adult psychiatry at the University of Illinois Neuropsychiatric Institute in Chicago, and in child and adolescent psychiatry at the Institute for Juvenile Research in Chicago. In 1975, he graduated from the Chicago Institute for Psychoanalysis with certificates in child and adult psychoanalysis.

He has taught at the University of Chicago School of Social Service Administration and in the Institute for Psychoanalysis adult and child psychotherapy programs. He is on the Board of Directors of the Intrapsychic Humanism Society.

Chapter One
Infants

♥

How should parents react when a newly mobile baby falls?

Q Our eight-month-old son is just learning to move around and has already had his share of rug burns and little tumbles. My husband and I aren't sure how to react to these falls. Though we've heard that overreacting and rushing to his side every time can cause him to cry at every little stumble, we also feel that simply telling him "You're okay," as he wails at the top of his lungs is a little extreme.

What is the proper way to react to a child's injury, especially when he's not old enough to voice the severity of it?

A Like so many parents, you have been misadvised that soothing your child's tears will harm him in some way. We cannot overemphasize the damage this advice has done to children. If you think about it, how can it make sense to treat children more harshly than you would treat a friend or than you would like to be treated? If you trip jogging and get pavement burns on your legs, you would undoubtedly prefer to have a friend or partner nearby to give you a sympathetic hug rather than to experience the pain alone. You would not entertain the idea that the soothing imparted by the hug would induce you to fall down again for the purposes of getting another hug. Presumably, if you want a hug from a friend or partner, all you have to do is to ask for it!

Similarly, when your son falls and cries, comforting him will have only positive consequences. By easing the trauma and upset he is feeling, you will help him to maintain his confidence and his desire to explore his environment. You also will show him the value of turning to a relationship for help and demonstrate the importance of helping others who are unhappy. And you will help him learn that while life has painful moments, he can count on your love and continue to feel loved and lovable when he is hurting. The notion that hugging and comforting your son will cause him to want to hurt himself again is utterly wrongheaded. If your son wants another hug, he knows that he can come to you and put his arms out. Why would he feel that he needed to be in pain in order to secure your affection?

On the other hand, if you follow the bad advice you were given and don't go to your child and comfort him when he falls, he will believe you want him to continue to suffer. He will learn not to expect help when he is unhappy. Eventually, he may convince himself that he doesn't want or need others, and he may lose the desire to help those who are hurting or in need.

So follow your excellent instincts. If your son falls and hurts himself, go to him and cuddle him, wipe away his tears, and give him the love that will fill his tank and motivate him to go back to his explorations certain that he is lovable, loving and loved.

Can too much love rattle nerves of newborn baby?

Q I have a six-week-old baby boy and a large extended family that lives nearby. I am the first of the "cousins" to have a child and so everyone comes by often to visit and admire my son. Everyone wants to hold him and I have been letting them. But I notice that after a lot of different people have held my son he has trouble getting to sleep and cries a lot. Do you think there really could be a connection between all the visitors and his unhappiness later or am I just making imaginary connections? My mother says my son is too young to notice or mind who is holding him.

A Your son is lucky to have a mother who is so attentive to his needs. Yes, your intuition is correct. Even at such a young age your son does know you and he can be upset by being held by so many strangers. There is convincing research showing that newborns can recognize their mother's voice, smell and touch and are calmed by her presence. It stands to reason, then, that when he is being held by strangers, a baby would notice and react to the absence of his mother. And if every time a baby gets used to the smell, touch and voice of one new person he is handed to another new person, it is easy to see that the baby's nerves could become quite jangled.

For now, let your family admire your son while he is held by you or your husband. After a few days, if it seems as though he is calm and sleeping better, you could try letting one new person a day hold him for a brief period.

Do babies need to understand "no?"

Q My husband and I have a disagreement about discipline. He believes that our eight-month-old son needs to learn the meaning of the word "no," so he plays a "game" with him by giving him a toy, book or other object, then taking it back and saying, "no." I can see that this upsets my son, but my husband tells me I'm just being too protective.

Is there anything to this idea that little children need to learn the meaning of the word "no" as early as possible? I hope he will listen to you, because he certainly won't listen to me.

A Your husband is completely misinformed about what your eight-month-old needs. Actually, he needs to hear "yes" as much as possible, and never "no."

As a baby, your son will experience having the toy taken from him and hearing "no" as a message that he has done something wrong and that your husband wants him to feel unhappy. Since, like all babies, he believes that his parents are perfect, he will assume that the unhappiness he feels when your husband interacts with him in this way is the way he is supposed to feel, and he will develop needs to recreate that unhappiness for himself and others. As he grows older, he may have trouble feeling that he deserves good feelings or good things. He is also learning a model of relating that involves tormenting others and he may copy that as well.

Babies do not need to learn the word "no." They need you lovingly to protect them from anything that can harm them. Making your son as happy as possible will not "spoil" him, but will facilitate his emotional development. He will copy your caring and grow up compassionate toward himself and others.

If after reading this, your husband feels it is necessary to keep playing this cruel and harmful game with your son, we advise you to get him to consult with a parenting counselor before he causes your son serious emotional harm.

Care and comfort after a cold?

Q My eight-month-old daughter recently had a week-long cold and fever. She is well now, but still wants the comforting and holding she got when she was sick. My friends with babies say that I should let her cry and not respond to her wish to be held because she is just spoiled from when she was sick and is manipulating me. What is your advice?

A It is a tragic and, sadly, a common misunderstanding to think that babies and young children who are expressing unhappiness or wishes for closeness are manipulating their parents. There is not a shred of scientific evidence indicating babies and young children are capable of faking unhappiness. When your daughter cries, she is genuinely unhappy at having her wish for closeness go unfulfilled; she is not manipulating you. You cannot "spoil" a child by responding to her wishes for love. Children who act "spoiled" have been deprived of real love and affection and given material things as (poor) substitutes. So they demand more material things than other children because they rely on these objects to feel a sense of inner well-being.

Your daughter's desire to be picked up and held is normal for a child her age, and also for a child who has been ill. Eight-month-olds are increasingly aware that their parents make them happiest of all. So it is natural they have intense feelings of wanting to be close. Gratifying this wish will make your daughter feel lovable and loved, thereby giving her the inner security she needs to blossom and develop. On the other hand, if you follow your friends' advice and refuse to pick her up when she asks, she will feel unloved and unlovable—undermining the confidence she needs to move on and explore. Finally, when babies have been ill, they often remain emotionally regressed for some time after their symptoms are gone. If parents are patient with their increased needs for love and affection, babies will return to their previous levels of confidence and independence. So follow your caring instincts and pick your daughter up when she asks for it. If you fill her tank now, her natural curiosity will return and inspire her to explore once again.

Is doctor right to say moms should leave the room?

Q I have to take my eight-month-old baby to the pediatrician for shots. A friend said her pediatrician advises mothers to stay outside the room during the shots so the baby doesn't blame the mother for the pain. I feel uneasy about letting my daughter go through the unpleasant experience without me, but I don't want my daughter to feel alienated from me. What are your thoughts about this?

A The irony is your daughter will blame you much more if you aren't there to comfort her when strangers are causing her pain. If the pain occurs in your absence, it will be that much worse because she will want you to be there to soothe her. In addition to the injection, she will have the pain of missing your calming presence. On the other hand, if you stay with her and hold her while the shot is administered and then do everything you can to comfort her, the pain will occur in the context of your love and warmth and will be quickly forgotten.

One other note—at eight months, your daughter is likely to suffer stranger anxiety, which means she may get upset when she sees a face other than yours. The "cure" for stranger anxiety is to reassure your daughter by letting her see your face. So this is an especially bad moment in her development to have strangers take her away from you and cause her pain. If you don't stay with her, the unpleasant experience may cause her to be abnormally vulnerable to stranger anxiety.

Learning to use utensils is important but messy

Q My eleven-month-old son wants to do everything we do, including eat with utensils. When I give him a spoon or fork he doesn't get much to eat and the food is all over him and the kitchen. But when I don't let him have utensils and he sees me eating with a fork and spoon he cries. I would like to wait until he is older, but I don't know how to make him accept that he can't have utensils now. Please help.

A Your son is going through an important developmental process. Unfortunately, you can't postpone it until a more convenient time. The most important engine powering successful development is the desire to be just like one's beloved parents. It is important to interfere with that motive as little as possible. Obviously your baby can't copy you and cook on the stove, but he can certainly try to eat with a child's fork and spoon.

You may feel better if you try to keep the mess to a minimum. Put a big plastic sheet under his high chair, dress him in something simple and washable, and let him have fun. If you are worried whether he is getting enough to eat, make sure he has some finger food on his tray and put some food on a separate spoon and offer it to him in between his own efforts. See if you can enjoy his pleasure at trying to master this skill and be grown up like Mom and Dad. Someday you may even look back on these meals with real nostalgia.

Our 5-month-old won't eat solids

Q Our pediatrician says it's time to start feeding our 5-month-old baby solids, but he's just not interested. We have tried different kinds of baby food, but he just makes a face and spits it out. He looks interested when we eat, but he can't have our food. How do we get him to eat solid food?

A You make a good observation when you say that your baby watches you eat. Imitation is one of the most powerful forces in child development, and you can use it to your advantage. Try "eating" food your son can have. Put some baby food in a bowl and give your son a spoon and take tastes out of it yourself. He will be much more likely to try new things if he sees you eating them.

To make it fun, give him the spoon. Put a plastic mat under his highchair so you aren't concerned about a mess. If he doesn't get too upset, try offering solid foods before milk. But pay attention to your son's signals. If he doesn't want a particular food, don't try to force it. Try something else at the next meal. The way to help your son become a good eater is to keep mealtimes pleasant and avoid power struggles.

♥

Our 13-month-old needs better table manners

Q My 13-month-old daughter has recently begun to throw food off her tray when she eats. She does this very defiantly, sometimes right after we tell her not to do that. It doesn't necessarily mean she's finished eating, because then she will start crying either for the thing she's just thrown on the floor or something else on the table.

We don't give her any food once she throws food off the tray. Both my husband and I are getting frustrated with the food throwing--not sure what she is trying to tell us, if anything.

How can we stop this food throwing?

A You are in a power struggle with a toddler. As every parent knows or discovers, toddlers' minds are different from adults'. Toddlers believe that they are all-powerful and also that they should be able to have and do whatever they want when they want. So when you tell your daughter not to throw food, she will throw it just to prove that she can.

Diplomacy and redirection work much better with toddlers than confrontation or negotiation. For example, put her high chair in the kitchen (assuming the floor is easily washed) and place small amounts of finger food she likes directly on the tray so there are no plates or cups to go flying. Then refrain from comment if she throws food on the floor. When she cries that she wants whatever she just threw, give her small amounts of new food. If she doesn't seem to want more food, simply take her out of the high chair and mop up the mess.

Once she realizes that you have stopped playing the food throwing game, she will too. Soon she will only throw food when she is finished eating. At that point, you can say (in a friendly way), "I see you are finished, let's get you down." Another approach is to distract her with toys, music or a story while she's eating. She may be so interested in these activities that she will only throw food as a sign she is no longer hungry.

If you opt out of the power struggle you are in, your daughter will throw food no more than other children her age, and will outgrow this behavior by about age three.

Should one-year-olds play alone?

Q My one-year-old never wants to sit and play alone. How do we help him to feel comfortable and do this?

A Your baby doesn't need to play alone. In fact, if he were to want to play alone for hours at a time, it would be a cause of concern. It is maturity, not weakness of character, that makes him want to be with you constantly. From a developmental standpoint, his feelings are entirely normal and appropriate. He is smart enough to realize you are the most fun of all, and needs to be responded to as positively as possible.

There is a mistaken notion that independence means distance and isolation from parents. Actually, true independence is freedom from needing externals such as good grades or material possessions to preserve a sense of inner well-being. In other words, babies whose wishes are granted whenever possible grow up so certain that they are loved and lovable, that their inner equilibrium becomes completely independent of life's successes and failures. So enjoy your baby's wish to be with you. Soon enough, he will be busy with a world of friends and school!

When friends clash over childcare philosophy

Q My husband and I juggle part-time jobs so we don't need childcare. Our best friends have a 10-month-old, and he is in a center 40 hours a week. Although we try, our friendship is in trouble because we cannot bear to hear about how wonderful the daycare is, and how much their baby enjoys it, etc. They are financially stable and (in my opinion) do not "need" two incomes. What should we do?

A Friendships are such precious assets, it would be a real shame to lose one because of a disagreement over the merits of daycare vs. stay-at-home parenting, especially when no one's opinion seems likely to change. Many people find it possible to remain close to friends whose views on important issues are very different from their own by avoiding "hot button" topics and agreeing to disagree. We suggest that you and your best friends make a similar pact about the childcare issue.

Why not decide that both couples will spend their time together discussing subjects that are mutually enjoyable? If your friends forget and begin to dwell on the benefits of daycare, you can remind them that you have all agreed to stay away from this topic in the interests of preserving your valuable friendship, then change the subject. Ask them to do the same for you.

Do I step-in or sit-by?

Q My ten-month-old is interested in putting blocks into her shape sorter. She can get the circle in, but when she tries the square or triangle, she gets frustrated after a few minutes and starts to cry. I always step in and help her, but my husband says I am not doing her a favor because in real life she will have to learn to cope with frustration. But it doesn't feel right to me to sit by and not help. What should I do?

A Your instincts are right on! The best way to ensure that children will grow up able to cope with frustration is to offer help when necessary. When parents don't aid young children who are unhappy and struggling, children learn that frustration is overwhelmingly painful and they try to avoid it by avoiding challenges. On the other hand, helping children when they are frustrated teaches them to approach difficult tasks with optimism and confidence that a solution can be found. We of course are not advocating that you step in and help children who are struggling but calm. The rule of thumb is, let children struggle as long as they feel determined and confident, but help them when they begin to feel miserable or like giving up.

Putting babies on eating and sleeping schedules

Q I am 8½ months pregnant with a girl and have been worrying about how to be a good mother to my baby. I want to get her off to a good start. Could you advise me on the best way to help her get on a good eating and sleeping schedule?

A To answer your question, we need first to address the larger issue: what is the real goal of parenting an infant? Understandably, new parents often worry most about short-term goals, such as correctly diapering or burping their baby. But the ultimate aim that should guide all the parenting you will do with your baby, including burping her, feeding her, responding to her tears and putting her to bed, is your desire to raise a happy, optimistic, caring, functional individual. The best way to achieve that goal is to do all of your parenting in a way that shows her that you love her and want her to be happy and not unhappy.

As we have often said, children adore their parents and learn to treat themselves exactly as their parents treat them, and this is why it is important not to focus on getting your baby to adhere to a particular eating or sleeping schedule. The reality is that babies are not naturally "scheduled." One day they may be very hungry and want lots of feedings, the next day they may eat much less. One day they may sleep many hours at night, the next day they may be awake most of the night.

Over time, infants' eating and sleeping schedules will become more predictable. It is true that you can rush a baby's natural cycle and force her to be on a regular schedule by letting her cry when she's hungry until it's time for the next meal or leaving her to cry in her crib until she falls asleep. Eventually, she will stop crying and appear to have learned to wait for food or to go to sleep on schedule. But in reality, she stops crying because she has stopped believing that she can get you to respond to her distress. She is conforming to a schedule that does not fit her needs out of a feeling of helplessness and hopelessness.

Babies' minds are different from adults' minds. Because she adores you and believes you are perfect, your baby believes that whatever she feels is what you intend for her to feel. If schedules are imposed on her and she feels helpless and unhappy, the lesson she will learn is that you don't respond to her tears because unhappiness is what you want for her. Because she thinks you are perfect, she will misidentify the unhappiness she feels as the good feelings you want her to have and she will learn to desire more of those "good" feelings, which are really unhappy feelings in disguise. This is obviously not the result parents have in mind when they think about putting their baby on a schedule, but it is the way the baby's mind works.

On the other hand, if you forget about trying to impose a schedule on your baby and respond to her tears (feed her when she is hungry, pick her up if she doesn't feel like sleeping), she will feel genuine happiness and she will conclude that this is the good feeling you want for her. She will learn to desire more of that happiness and will grow into a compassionate person who fosters happiness in others. Rather than developing feelings of hopelessness and helplessness, she will feel confident and optimistic. You can see, then, that forgetting about schedules and making your baby as contented and comfortable as possible is the best and, in fact, the only way to attain your long term goal of helping her to become a happy, caring human being.

Getting babies to sleep alone?

Q Where do you stand on the issue of getting kids to sleep on their own and sleep through the night? My five-month-old sleeps on her own mattress next to our bed (both are on the floor) and lately, after she nurses, she won't go back to sleep and keeps me up. I'm tired and I'm starting to want some privacy with my husband back. But I don't know how to move her out of our room or get her to sleep through the night without making her "cry it out," which I don't want to do. What's your approach?

A Whether or not parents keep young children in the same bed or the same room with them is really a matter of personal preference, as there are obvious advantages and disadvantages on both sides. You mention two of the disadvantages, namely that babies are often restless sleepers and keep parents awake, and that nighttime is one of the few times parents have to be alone together.

In general, if you decide that you want your child to sleep in her own room, it is probably better to help her to learn to put herself to sleep in her own room before she gets much older. After about six months of age, she will be much more aware of her surroundings and will resist a room change much more vigorously than she will now.

We applaud your reluctance to let your daughter "cry it out." Babies who are left to cry themselves to sleep fall asleep convinced that their parents want them to feel unhappy. Because they want to be just like their parents, they can develop needs to make themselves and others unhappy. Yet there is a way to help your daughter make the transition to sleeping in a separate room without traumatizing her. When she seems sleepy, place her on a mattress or in a crib in "her" room. If she cries, stay with her and talk to her and stroke her until she falls asleep. Try to comfort her while she remains in her bed. If she becomes so upset that you need to pick her up, calm her down and then put her down again. If you remain patient and soothing, she will eventually fall asleep. Over a few days' time, she will grow to accept and like her new quarters. Most important, she will know that you care about her and want to help her when she is upset and she will grow up to care for herself and to be compassionate to others.

Are we damaging our baby by letting him cry himself to sleep?

Q My husband and I are attempting to teach our five-month-old boy to put himself to sleep. We lay him down and let him cry, but we go in every five and seven minutes and tell him we love him. What kind of damage are we doing when we let him cry?

A You're so right to be alarmed about the negative side effects of letting a baby cry himself to sleep! There is a popular but unrealistic and, ultimately, harmful notion that infants should not bother their parents at night and that responding positively to babies who are having trouble sleeping teaches them to take advantage of their parents' caring and deprives parents of sleep on a regular basis.

Anyone who advises you to let your baby cry until he gives up and falls asleep is focusing on the baby's behavior (going to sleep all alone) and not on how the baby feels in the process. The problem is that when infants are left to cry themselves to sleep, they are forced to conclude that they are not lovable enough to engage their parents' desires to comfort them. If they actually stop crying, it is because they have abandoned all hope that help will come. The meaningful question, then, is not, "What will make my baby go to sleep with the least attention?" but, "What will enable my baby to put himself to sleep with the self-confidence that comes from feeling happy and cared about?"

If you offer your baby relationship pleasure rather than relationship deprivation, you will help him go to sleep secure in the conviction that you love him and want him to be happy. You can put him down when you think he's sleepy, sing to him, rub his tummy, or find other ways to comfort him, and then leave the room. If he cries, you can return and calm him and then leave again.

Although in the first year you may have to return many times to your baby's crib to rock him, give him the breast or bottle, or stroke him, your baby will learn that you can be relied on to respond to his needs and also that he can put himself to sleep in a contented manner (and not out of despair). Over time, as your baby learns that his cries will be responded to, he will need less input from you to feel comforted and sleep.

A baby who is responded to in this way will become a child who is a sound and reliable sleeper; and you will be rewarded with many peaceful nights as the result of your efforts in your baby's first year. Sleep-deprived parents of crying babies often feel very tempted to let their infants cry themselves to sleep so that they, themselves, will be able to get some rest. We ourselves know from experience how exhausted parents of infants can become. But we also know that you will be repaid later for the extra effort you make for your baby now. Your baby cannot perceive that you are tired and need peace and quiet, so when he is left to cry himself to sleep he has to think that you are choosing to leave him feeling helpless and miserable.

What's the secret to putting a baby to bed without crying?

Q Could you please explain the steps of putting a 3-month-old baby to sleep without just letting the baby cry? We like your approach, but we are having a problem implementing it. Our son tends to fall asleep after he has his bottle and when we put him down, he wakes up and wants to be held or rocked. How do you get babies to put themselves to sleep without letting them cry or having to hold and rock them forever?

A Your goal is to put your son in his crib awake and with enough interesting toys to keep him engaged until he falls asleep. If he falls asleep before you can put him in the crib, but then wakes up, try to comfort him in the crib. He will be more willing to stay in the crib if there are new and different things to look at in his crib. In the beginning, he may become tired and want some comforting after playing. Try to rub his back or soothe him without picking him up. If he becomes upset, lift him up, rock and comfort him and then try to put him down again and comfort him in the crib. Over time, you will find that more frequently he will play for a while and then fall asleep.

Am I being too permissive?

Q My husband and I have been following the advice in *Smart Love* since the interview in *Chicago Parent* in May. It really flows with your instinct to parent. I am having trouble sometimes distinguishing between *Smart Love* and permissiveness.

On the one hand *Smart Love* calls for you to do everything you can to keep your child happy and comfortable, but yet if you allow them to be happy on their own terms, you may be responding permissively, teaching them that their all powerful selves are too strong to be interfered with.

At what point is loving regulation applied? Example: Our 11½-month-old daughter goes to bed rather late but sleeps in as well which is fine with me and my schedule. My husband feels she should be going to bed earlier but my argument is that she isn't tired. When put to bed earlier, she will be content alone in her crib for awhile, eventually becoming unhappy. Going in again and again for reassurance causes her crying to escalate to the point of having to pick her up. Is loving regulation needed or should she be able to stay up until she's ready to sleep? Thank you.

A You don't say whether one or both of you is working, but often when parents work, children want to stay up later in order to have more time with them. Whatever the reason, if your daughter is "sleeping in" in the morning, she is getting enough sleep even though she may be getting to bed later than her peers.

Since her sleeping schedule fits with your lifestyle, you are absolutely correct to conclude that there is no reason to cause conflict by trying to change a pattern that makes her happy and comfortable. This is not permissiveness, because you are not letting her do something that is harmful to herself or others or that is otherwise not in her best interest. Permissiveness would be letting her stay up late when she had to be up early in the morning, with the result that she would be robbed of much-needed sleep.

Loving regulation is used when you must interfere with a child's behavior, usually because it is potentially harmful to the child, to others, or to property. Loving regulation is a way of being in charge of your child without adding unpleasant consequences, including lectures, time-outs, restriction of privileges, and spanking. For example, if your daughter were trying to touch the stove, you would stop her in a friendly way (for example, get out her play stove or, if you don't need to be in the kitchen, go with her to another room and start an enjoyable activity). By using loving regulation you show your child that even when she can't have what she wants, she can always have a loving relationship with you. That knowledge will actually make her more resilient and less dependent on getting what she wants when she wants it as she grows older.

Can my seven-month-old go to sleep without crying?

Q My seven-month-old has a lot of difficulty going down to sleep both at night and for naps. He is very unhappy about being put in his crib and even more unhappy when I walk out of the room. I come back in when he protests. He is fine when I sit by his bed, but every time I leave it's the same thing. It is taking me an hour or two to get him to bed. I know he's tired, but he just doesn't seem able to fall asleep. I know you don't advocate leaving children to cry, but what do you advise us to do?

A There is all the difference in the world between leaving children to cry themselves to sleep, which for reasons we have discussed in previous columns is harmful to children, and allowing children the space to protest and be grumpy and unhappy about being put to bed. Seven-month-olds have no more notion of being tired and needing sleep than they do of needing to be in their car seats. Moreover, they love being awake and interacting with the adults who mean everything to them. So it is understandable that being put to bed can make them feel very out of sorts. However, young children need sleep even when they don't think they do.

What you need to do is to establish a bedtime ritual and then differentiate between crying miserably and complaining. Make certain that your son is really tired. Then develop a pattern around putting him to bed that he will find soothing. For example, give him some milk, look at a book together, sing him a song, and then put him into his crib with his favorite blanket or animals, say "night, night" and leave the room. Then listen carefully to him. It is normal for him to complain and protest a bit. Baby complaints are often expressed as grunts or angry-sounding vocalizations. The complaining baby sounds put-out—not scared or hysterical. Crying is different. The baby will gasp for air and may sound miserable, frightened or hysterical as well. As long as your son is complaining and occasional crying sounds don't last for more than a minute or two, there is no harm in letting him figure out how to put himself to sleep.

Inevitably babies and young children will feel unhappy at times because their immaturity leads them to want things they can't have (to stay up too late, to play with sister's violin). The challenge for you as a parent is to distinguish between leaving your child alone when he is miserably unhappy (which will harm him) and allowing him to protest and express anger when he has to do something he wouldn't choose at that moment. Like every other aspect of parenting, making this distinction will be easier with practice.

♥

Baby wears out parents

Q My four-week-old baby doesn't seem to distinguish between night and day. She is most awake from about midnight to 3:00 a.m. and does her best sleeping during the day. My pediatrician advises me to get her on a schedule by putting her in her crib at night and letting her cry herself to sleep. I know you argue against leaving babies to cry, but I am exhausted from lack of sleep and really want my baby to get night and day straightened out. Do you have any suggestions that don't involve leaving her to cry?

A Your baby is in the very early stages of adjusting to life outside the uterus. Perhaps you are expecting her to sleep longer at night than she can at this point. This is a very short-term problem—when you look at it from the perspective of 21 or so years of growing up.

You are right that letting her cry is not the way to teach her to sleep better at night. The emotional price babies pay for being left to cry is to think that the unhappiness they feel is what their parents want for them. They then develop the need to recreate those same unhappy feelings for themselves.

We know how tired parents of newborns can be, but if you comfort your baby when she has difficulty sleeping you will reap the future reward of seeing your baby become a calm, confident, optimistic child.

That said, we do have some practical suggestions for hastening the process by which your baby learns to sleep at night and play during the day. First, try to be as boring as possible between 10:00 p.m. and 5:00 a.m. Of course, you always want to use a caring, gentle touch, but try to avoid stimulating your baby. Don't turn on more lights than necessary, don't be too talkative, don't bring the baby into a room with a lot of activity or other people, don't leave anything but a small night light on at night. During her daytime naps, leave the lights on or the windows uncovered. In the not too distant future, your baby will respond and begin to differentiate night and day. Meanwhile, whenever possible let the chores go and sleep when your baby sleeps so as to preserve your own strength.

Ferberizing babies

Q Would you please revisit the topic of Ferberizing babies? I have a four-month-old who wakes up twice a night. He doesn't seem that hungry, but he really cries if I don't go to him and feed him. Then he is content and goes back to sleep.

When I tell my friends how tired I am, they all tell me to let him cry—that the first few times are hard, but that after that he will sleep through the night. I know you don't think it's good to let babies cry, but I need my sleep too. Please advise.

A The trouble with "Ferberizing" babies is not that it doesn't "work," in the sense of making the baby sleep through the night, but that it interferes with the baby's emotional development and puts the baby's long-term well-being at risk. If your only goal were to get your baby to sleep through the night and not bother you, then leaving him to cry would accomplish that goal. The problem, however, is that the reason the Ferberized baby stops crying and goes to sleep is that he becomes so discouraged that he gives up trying to signal that he needs help. In effect, he has learned to sleep through the night out of despair rather than out of contentment.

We emphasize that it is entirely normal for a baby to wake up during the night. Babies grow and mature at different rates and have delicate digestive systems; they may wake up because they are hungry, because their tummies are bothering them, or for some other reason. Once they are awakened, they may feel lonely and want a little comforting. These are all perfectly sensible reasons to go to them and soothe them.

You say that when you go to your son and feed him, he goes back to sleep contented. By responding to him, you are not only keeping him comfortable and allowing him to go back to sleep happy rather than despairing, but you are also giving him the crucial message that you care that he is unhappy and that you will do what you can to help him feel better. Because he loves you and wants to be exactly like you, your responsiveness is teaching him to be a person who is compassionate toward himself and others.

On the other hand, babies whose tears go uncomforted also emulate their parents. They believe that since their parents are not responding to them, they don't deserve comfort when they are upset. They may well grow up lacking compassion toward their own or others' upset feelings. Worse, because they believe that their uncomforted feelings are what they are supposed to feel, they can confuse this unhappiness with happiness and develop the need to make themselves unhappy.

So continue to be responsive to your son's tears. If you are tired, get someone to take over for you for an hour during the day so you can rest, or nap when he naps and let the chores go. In the long run, you will be well compensated for the sleep you lose because you will be helping your son to grow up to be a happy and caring adult.

What can I do about a baby who won't sleep through the night?

Q I have a seven-week-old who is an adorable healthy baby. Our only problem is that she doesn't seem to sleep as long at night as my friends' babies. I have read your reasons not to let babies cry themselves to sleep and agree with them, but I wonder what we can do to help her (and us) get more sleep at night without damaging her emotional development.

A Our first suggestion is to stop comparing your baby to your friends' babies! Your baby may be waking up hungry because she is in a growing spurt or she didn't burp well at the last feeding and stopped eating before she was full. Or she may wake because she is wet or otherwise uncomfortable. In other words, your baby has a good reason for waking and she needs to have her needs met no matter what time of day they are expressed.

That said, there are ways to respond at night that can help your baby get back to sleep quickly and, eventually, help her to put herself back to sleep if she wakes but isn't hungry or uncomfortable.

When you go to your baby at night, be caring but *boring*. Don't turn on more lights than you absolutely need to see what you are doing. Hold the baby lovingly and do what has to be done, but talk to her as little as possible and don't stimulate her in any other way. You have the rest of the day to hold "conversations," to engage her attention with mobiles that turn and make music, to sing to her, or to give her a kiss. By not stimulating her unnecessarily at night, you are showing her that night is a time for sleeping and not for partying.

How do I get my baby's sleep schedule back to normal?

Q Our 6-month-old is really having a hard time sleeping. He was doing pretty well—waking up only once a night—until we went on vacation. Then he started waking up three or four times a night and having trouble going back to sleep.

My husband and I are exhausted. It ruined our vacation, and now that we are back home he is still not on a good schedule. My pediatrician told us to let him cry himself to sleep, but I agree with you that doing so is harmful. Suggestions?

A Six months is typically the time when babies become more aware of their surroundings and prefer to sleep in their own rooms and cribs. They often have trouble sleeping in new places and readjusting to their old rooms.

One solution is to have crib bumpers, mobiles, music and toys that you take with you to every new location, even for naps, so your son will have some degree of familiarity. Another strategy is to have nap and bedtime rituals, such as feeding him, followed by laying him down and singing a special song. These cues will help him fall asleep in strange situations.

We are certain that since your son was sleeping well before your trip, once he gets used to his home base again, he will return to his good sleep habits.

My daughter is not sleeping, neither am I

Q I read a reply you gave someone else about not letting a baby cry herself to sleep. I agreed with everything you had to say. However, my fouteen-month-old is waking up every hour at night. Finally after dawn she will sleep for two hours. I don't want to ignore her, and I can't, but I'm getting run down from lack of sleep and I don't think it's good for her either. Is this sleep anxiety? I'm still breastfeeding and that's the only thing that will get her back to sleep. Help!

A At fourteen months, your daughter should be sleeping more than an hour or two at a time, and we can understand how tired you must be. There are a number of possible explanations but you will have to experiment to discover which ones are most relevant to your daughter. You mention you are breastfeeding, but it is not clear whether your daughter is also eating solid foods. If not, it is possible she is hungry and why she sleeps after being breastfed. Talk to your pediatrician.

Or maybe you are responding too quickly when your daughter

wakes. Babies and young children actually wake up a number of times every night and often fall back to sleep after a few minutes of complaining or rustling around. While we do not recommend that you let your daughter cry without comforting her, if you hear her in the night, you might try waiting until you are certain she is really crying. If it becomes necessary to intervene, do your best not to stimulate your daughter. Leave the lights off, don't play with her or talk to her more than necessary—in other words, be as boring as possible while you feed or change her in order to keep her from waking fully.

Also, evaluate your daughter's sleeping environment. Is there too much light? Is her room too hot or too cold? Is she over- or underdressed?

One of these should do the trick—if not, we recommend you have your pediatrician do a complete evaluation to be sure there are no medical reasons for her sleep disruptions.

Should children sleep with lights and music?

Q I value your input and have heard a lot of pros and cons, but what is your feeling about young children using music (soft & otherwise) and/or night lights to aid them in falling asleep? Do these things really aid infants or serve more as a crutch as they grow older?

A Unlike pacifiers and bottles, which can damage teeth, there is no downside whatsoever to using music or night lights to help children sleep.

The transition to sleep is difficult for most children. They enjoy being awake and hate to give up whatever enjoyable activities they are doing. And young children can feel painfully out of sorts when they get overtired. So if your child is helped to sleep by music or night lights, that's wonderful.

Sometimes young children also like cloth books, mobiles or other toys that are safe to sleep with. Children experience all of these things as substitutes for their parents. Having them around makes children feel loved and cared for. As children grow older, their inner happiness will not diminish at bedtime, and they will no longer need music or night lights to get to sleep peacefully. So make your child as comfortable as possible going to bed now, and don't worry about his needing music and a night light as an adult!

Help. My five-month-old needs to be held day and night

Q I have a five-month-old son. He is my third child. I am having two problems, both connected I think. For the last five weeks or so he has wanted to be held pretty much all day. Needless to say, I can't do that and at times he just cries and cries. When I nurse him, he falls asleep but only takes quick catnaps because when he wakes up, he can't get himself back to sleep. This can go on all day; I can get nothing done. I am lucky if I can get my other two children lunch.

I am exhausted and resentful by the end of the day and too tired to do the things I need to do. I have some outside help for a few hours a week, and my husband is supportive, but I need to break my son of this habit. I am a firm believer in not letting babies cry — my other two children are very secure and confident, so I know letting him cry is not the right thing. The night is not much better. If he wakes up he needs to be held to go to sleep. Some nights he sleeps ten hours, and some nights he is up after five.

A It sounds as though you are pretty swamped with caregiving responsibilities. But your five-month-old is being a baby and acting his age — he is not trying to manipulate you or make your life miserable. Not holding him simply makes him more miserable and more desperate for the comfort he wants. Wanting to be held is not a bad habit that needs to be broken. If your baby wants to be held, then he needs to be held.

For whatever reason, he is feeling upset and he is turning to you because you are the light of his life and his best source of comfort. If you need your hands free more of the time, you could put him in a baby sling and carry him that way. We are convinced that if you respond to the needs he is expressing and hold him as much as possible, soon he will feel more confident of your love and more comforted and he will begin to spend some pleasurable time enjoying his toys.

♥

My baby wakes up hungry every night. What do I do?

Q We need help with our 4-month-old baby. She goes to sleep OK around 8:30 p.m., but then wakes up at 1 a.m. and 4 a.m. wanting a bottle. She goes back to sleep, but I have trouble getting back to sleep and am exhausted during the day. I can't ask my husband for help because he works with heavy machinery and it would be dangerous for him to be tired. My pediatrician suggested I not feed my daughter a whole bottle when she wakes up because she will learn to expect it. Instead, the doctor said I should let her cry for a while when she wakes up. But when I let her cry and then give her only half a bottle, she gets hysterical and won't go back to sleep for an hour—and I get even less sleep. What do you suggest?

A You have our sympathies for your lack of sleep. But there is no magic answer except to wait for your baby to mature. As she gets older, she will be able to get by on one bottle a night and eventually will sleep all the way through. As long as she wakes up wanting a bottle, she is hungry and needs to be fed. You are doing the right thing, because letting her cry or go hungry is not good for her emotionally or physically. As you have seen, giving her less milk than she wants only makes her more upset. The trouble is that without a partner who can take turns, you are wearing out. Perhaps another family member would be willing to spend the night and take on the feedings once in awhile. Or perhaps your husband could take the night feedings on weekends. Another suggestion is to use your baby's daytime naps to nap yourself—elective chores take second place to your need for rest.

We're divorcing: When will our 13-month-old be ready to sleep away from his home?

Q We are getting a divorce and planning how to share parenting of our 13-month-old son, Noah. We are both committed to having Mom continue to work only two evenings a week, so our son will almost always be with either his mother or father. Noah will sleep at his mother's home for the time being. At what point, developmentally, will our son be ready to spend 24 hours or more away from his mother and his primary residence (i.e., at his father's home)

A Divorce, no matter how rational, can be terribly stressful, and we are impressed that in this trying time you are both able to put your child's interests first. And you're absolutely right to feel that for now, it is better for Noah to sleep at home with his primary caregiver, his mom.

Noah is developmentally in a phase of separation anxiety. Separation anxiety appears between nine and twelve months of age and may last until the child is two or two-and-a-half. Separation anxiety is the age-appropriate and temporary loss of well-being that is triggered by the absence of the baby's primary caregiver or caregivers. Noah will be less likely to feel separation anxiety from his mother when he is with his dad than when he is with other adults. But no baby is at his best at the end of the day, and at that point being with his primary caregiver in his own room with his favorite things will make it easier for him to get to sleep comfortably.

We recommend that you continue to use Noah's comfort as your guide. When Noah becomes comfortable taking his nap at his dad's house, try letting him spend the night. Bring along his favorite portable comforts, and get a crib that is as similar as possible to the one he has at home. If he seems distressed or has trouble sleeping when he spends the night with Dad, wait another month or two and try again. By waiting until Noah is ready for overnights at Dad's, you give him the invaluable knowledge that, although his parents may not be living together, they remain united in their concern for his welfare. And your sensitivity to your son's developmental needs for stability and familiarity represents the informed love that will allow him to grow up feeling confident, worthwhile, and effective.

If I care for my grandchild half-time, will she confuse me with her mother?

Q I'm a young grandmother—36 years old. The mother of my grandchild is my son's 16-year-old girlfriend. She has been living here for over a year. Everyone gets along well. My granddaughter is 2 months old. I care for this child at least half the time (which I love to do). But could the baby get confused about who her mother is? The mother is a very good mother, but she still must finish school, I insist upon it! She is an A student now, and I help because I want to, not have to. I just don't want to screw things up.

A The two younger generations of your family are so fortunate to have such a caring and dedicated mother/grandmother! Your constructive, nonpunitive attitude toward your son and his girlfriend is immensely enriching their lives and the life of their baby.

You needn't worry that you are confusing the baby by caring for her half-time. The baby knows and loves her mother just as she will know and love her grandmother. You're performing the invaluable service of helping the mother of your grandchild finish her education while ensuring that the baby never lacks a loving, supportive, reliable relationship. The time the baby has with her mother will give her an ample experience of her mother's love and commitment. And the stable, loving care she receives from you will actually strengthen the baby's bonds to her parents. Since, like all babies, your granddaughter is convinced that her parents are perfect caregivers who design every aspect of her world, she will give her parents a lot of the credit for the good times she has with you. Keep up your wonderful work!

Will having a second child too soon hurt my son?

Q Could you address the issue of spacing children? I have a thirteen-month-old and have been thinking about getting pregnant again. I can see that my son needs me a lot right at the moment, but I assume that he would be ready for a sibling when he is around two. On the other hand, I have friends who have had second children when their first was around two and they have found it very difficult to cope. My thirteen-month-old is very happy and easygoing, so I am hoping that it won't be a problem.

A Ideally, it is best to space children at least three years apart. Until children are about three, they are too immature to know that their parents love them even when they can't immediately respond to them.

As a result, children under three find it very difficult to wait when they want attention and their parents are occupied elsewhere (as with a younger sibling). Once they turn three, children who have been adequately responded to pass a developmental milestone. In most cases they are able to wait for their parents' attention, secure in the knowledge that their parents love them and want to spend time with them as soon as possible. This is the reason three-year-olds cope better with new siblings than do younger children.

This said, we recognize that many parents need to have their children close together and also that sometimes babies just come along when the next oldest sibling is under three. Parents who have two children under three should keep in mind that it is normal for the older child to chafe at the time spent with the new arrival and should make sure that they set aside sufficient time to spend alone with the older child. If the older child can enjoy the warmth of having his parents' undivided attention for some part of every day, his emotional development will proceed normally and he will not become unduly resentful of the new sibling.

What do we need to know about parenting twins?

Q To my amazement, my husband and I find ourselves the parents of fraternal girl twins, now four months old. So far so good, but I am wondering if we need to be thinking about parenting them differently than single children. We are getting all kinds of conflicting advice from friends and neighbors

A It is better to think of parenting twins as caring for two children the same age rather than as caring for children that are alike. When children are spaced a year or more apart, parents don't tend to assume that they will share personality traits; the same mind-set should prevail with twins.

In practical terms that means, for example, that the twins may be on completely different schedules for feeding or sleeping and they may have very different likes and dislikes. The more you can be sensitive to each child's individual needs, the fewer problems you will have, because each child will feel loved for herself rather than as part of a unit. At the same time, don't force them to be different – if they both like doing the same activity at the same time, that is fine as well.

The same principle applies when it is time for them to go to school. If they get along famously and love being together, they might enjoy being in the same classroom. If they fight constantly, they would probably benefit from being in different classes. In short, if you approach your girls as individuals and are guided by their interests and preferences, they will enter adulthood experiencing themselves as individuals first and twins second.

Should a baby be smiling by 7 weeks?

Q My sister-in-law is worried about her 7-week-old baby girl who isn't smiling yet. Should she be worried, and what can she do?

A You and your sister-in-law are certainly right to think of a baby's smile as a barometer of how she is feeling about herself and the world, but 7 weeks is too soon to worry because a baby hasn't smiled yet. The first social smile may appear as early as 6 weeks, but it's unlikely to be a regular feature for quite a while. Generally, babies will smile readily by 12 weeks, and, by 6 months, they smile most ecstatically at the people they know best.

In the highly unlikely event that your niece does not smile by the time she is 3-months-old, first have her checked by her pediatrician to make certain that she is not being made uncomfortable by a physiological problem. Most babies over 3 months of age who are in a familiar setting with familiar people and toys—and who are not ill or overtired—will smile readily.

Though, of course, no baby feels like smiling every time she is smiled at, if as a 3-month-old this baby still seems "serious" most of the time, ask yourselves whether:

- The baby is being overstimulated by too much tickling, bouncing, etc.
- The baby is being left to play alone for long periods without seeing a smiling, loving adult face or being gently held.
- The baby has a babysitter or is in daycare, and the people caring for her are not giving her enough positive attention.

In all probability, though, if you just continue to love and cherish your niece, her smile will dawn any day now.

She coos, you coo, we all coo

Q I have a three-month-old daughter who just started cooing. What is the best way to respond to her to encourage her to "speak" to me? Should I imitate her sounds or say something different in "my" language? A friend says that if you respond in "baby talk," the baby will never learn to talk. Thanks for helping.

A The most important thing to teach your baby about "talking" is that it's fun. And your baby will have the most fun when you talk in her language. Research has shown there is a good reason for talking baby talk to babies; they learn from simple sounds and speech and are stimulated to vocalize more and more.

When your baby coos to you, coo right back. At first, it's best to try to imitate her. You will find that when she makes a cooing sound and you copy it immediately, she will be spellbound. She will be amazed at her ability to get you to respond to her sounds and inspired to make more of them. Some babies are happiest if you limit your responses to their sounds, others like it when you imitate them and add new sounds for them to try. Keep your talks pleasurable. It's not what you say but your baby's enjoyment of relating to you that will stimulate her to talk.

Is picking up a crying baby spoiling a child?

Q I really enjoy your column and now I need some advice myself. I am very confused about whether and how long to let my baby cry. My pediatrician says that if we respond immediately when she cries, the baby will learn to cry in order to get attention. He recommends that unless we know she is dirty or really hungry, that we wait at least five minutes to see if she will stop on her own. He says that if we pick her up right away, she will turn into a child who cries at the drop of a hat. Yet I really hate letting her cry for five minutes before comforting her. It seems that during that five minutes her crying escalates rather than dies down and often when I go to her she is sobbing and hysterical. What is your perspective on this? Should we respond differently at different times, such as at night or during the day?

A Actually, it's not true either that babies cry to get attention or that they will learn to cry longer or more frequently if they are responded to immediately. Babies cry for one reason only—they are unhappy. The causes of unhappiness can range from hunger, to needing a diaper change, feeling ill, being in pain, being overstimulated, being understimulated, being overtired and so on. The reality is that when you follow your good instincts and respond immediately to your crying baby, she will actually cry less, because she becomes increasingly confident that her cries will bring help. Empirical studies have shown that if a baby is picked up within 90 seconds of beginning to cry, the crying lasts an average of five seconds. Babies who are not picked up within 90 seconds cry for 50 seconds or more. Responsiveness is just as important at night as in the daytime. Babies who awake at night and are left to cry become much more aroused and have more difficulty going back to sleep than babies who are comforted immediately. So enjoy soothing your baby at any time of the day or night in the knowledge that you are helping, not harming, her.

Is it possible for a baby to be spoiled?

Q I am the mother of a four-month-old and my instinct is to try to comfort her when she is unhappy and to keep her as happy as possible. But both my mother and my mother-in law are telling me that I will spoil her. Is it possible to spoil a baby?

A Bravo for your instincts! Contrary to what the baby's grandmothers are telling you, compassion will never spoil a baby (or an older child, either). Like all babies, your baby entered the world convinced that you are a perfect parent giving her ideal care. Your responsiveness is the measure your baby uses to gauge her self-worth. Gratifying your child's wishes, especially for comfort and attention, will not spoil your child. It will not make her hopelessly self-centered or unable to postpone gratification.

On the contrary, your child's all-encompassing need for your focused caring will decrease when she becomes certain of your unconditional wish to respond. Your child will learn that life is such that she cannot always have the things she wants, but she can always have a positive, loving response from you. When you try to make her as happy as possible and soothe her cries, you sustain her inborn optimism and give her an inner well-being rich enough to share with others.

In reality, "spoiled" children behave in ways that antagonize adults because they have received too little positive attention, not too much. Parents are sometimes told that their baby is trying to manipulate them when she cries, but manipulation is a word that never applies to babies. Assertions about the infant's wily motives are disproved by scientific evidence; the data conclusively contradict the notion that infants can fake unhappiness.

Crying is not a calculated act. Babies cry because they feel overwhelmed and need your loving assistance. When their parents do not respond to their tears, babies find themselves in a vicious circle:

they feel unlovable when they are unhappy, and they are unhappy because they feel unlovable.

On the other hand, because you are the source of your young child's greatest joy, when you freely supply your loving attention, you give your baby a storehouse of well-being that will last a lifetime and make her strong and resilient by seeing her through every disappointment and frustration.

Is it manipulation when baby throws toys?

Q My 10-month-old is going through a period of throwing every toy out of his crib, then bursting into tears and becoming hysterical because he doesn't have them anymore. But when we give the toys back to him, he immediately cheers up and throws them out again.

When we tire of this game, he gets so hysterical that he has even thrown up. My friends tell me I shouldn't give in because he is manipulating us. What do you think?

A Many babies go through this phase. The bad news is that it can be quite demanding on parents. The good news is that your child will outgrow it.

You have to remember your baby's mind is different from yours. He enjoys his new ability to throw the toys, and doesn't realize that once he throws them, they are gone. So when the toys just lie there, he understandably feels frustrated. If you don't help, he feels angry with you. He is not manipulating you—rather, he is expressing frustration. By retrieving the toys, you show him that you want to respond to his needs for help.

Soon your son will realize that when he throws toys out of his crib, he can't reach them. Then he will no longer throw the toys he wants, only the ones he is tired of, and will become less insistent you retrieve them.

How do I prepare my baby for house guests?

Q We are having a family reunion and loads of family are going to be staying with us or coming to the house. My 7-month-old is showing signs of stranger anxiety, and I am worried that she will be upset by all the new faces. Some of my husband's relatives have never seen the baby. I know they will want to pick her up, but I am not sure she will like that. I don't want to hurt our guests' feelings, but it won't be good if the baby melts down either. How can we keep everyone happy?

A Your are correct in assuming that a deluge of strange relatives may be overwhelming. The best solution is for you or your husband to make sure that you are near her—even holding her if possible. Let her greet the new arrivals from the safety of your arms or your lap. If well-meaning relatives want to pick your baby up, tell them that she is in a normal phase of being a little hesitant with people she doesn't know well. Suggest that the relatives talk to her or play peek-a-boo without actually holding her. In that way, both your relatives and your daughter will have a mutually enjoyable experience.

Should I pass my infant around to all my visitors?

Q Three weeks ago, I gave birth to a son, the first grandchild on either side of the family. Understandably, everyone wants to come and see and hold the baby. I am beside myself with happiness at having this gorgeous baby and selfishly hate to hand him over. Also, I wonder whether it's good for so many people to hold him. I don't want to be a party pooper. At the same time, I feel a little overwhelmed and uncertain what is best for my son.

A First, we suggest that you control the number of visitors each day. You and your husband need time to enjoy your son and to help him feel comfortable and happy. You can establish one or two regular times when people can come over, then limit the number of visitors. If a friend or relative calls on a busy day, you can say, "We would love to see you, but today isn't good—how about tomorrow at 7 p.m.?

Second, people often assume that babies are too immature to distinguish between people and that they can be handed from person to person without a problem. Research shows, however, that newborns recognize their parents' voices and mother's smell and are comforted by them.

Babies also recognize strange stimuli. As a result, they can have difficulty relaxing and sleeping if they are passed from person to person. Conversely, they tend to remain relaxed and adapt well to new experiences when they are held by familiar people. So instead of passing your son around, take him with you and sit next to your visitors so they can hold his tiny hand and look into his face while he is in your arms. That way your visitors will have an up-close experience with your son while he remains in the security of your arms, smell and voice.

Why is my baby rejecting me?

Q I am the hardworking father of a 7-month-old girl. My job takes me on the road Monday through Friday. I don't have much energy left for playing with the baby, but I get a lot of satisfaction from being a good provider for my family.

The last two weekends, I have gone in to get my daughter up from her nap and she has looked at me and burst into tears. She has remained inconsolable until my wife picks her up. My feelings are hurt and I wonder why I am working so hard and traveling so much when my daughter clearly seems not to like having me around. Should I just insist that she accept me and not let my wife step in? Please advise.

A Your baby has reached a normal, time-limited developmental stage called stranger anxiety. She has matured to the point that she can distinguish the person she gets the most comfort from—her mother—from everyone else. She doesn't see you every day, so for the moment, you are not the person who feels most familiar and most comforting.

This is a normal and time-limited reaction that has no implications for your future relationship with your daughter. Very soon, her development will continue to the point that she will include you in her "favorite" category. And when she reaches the romantic phase, which occurs sometime around age 3, she will go through a normal phase of preferring you and on occasion, rejecting her mother.

In order not to interfere with the normal unfolding of your daughter's development, it is important that you understand this developmental stage and realize your daughter is not rejecting you when she cries; she is simply expressing a normal preference for the person who spends the most time with her.

If you can be sensitive to this developmental vulnerability, you will find that your relationship will be smoother. For example, if you want to get her up from her nap, go in with her mother and let her see her mother's face as you pick her up. With that security in place, she will probably be very comfortable playing with you.

Why is my eight-month-old suddenly acting unfriendly and antisocial?

Q My eight-month-old baby, who has always been happy and outgoing, has become suddenly unfriendly. When her grandparents come to visit, or we meet neighbors in the elevator, she no longer smiles at their advances but looks solemn and even cries sometimes. I am worried that I am doing something wrong and my baby is becoming depressed or antisocial. Is there something I should be doing to make her happier?

A Your daughter's suspicious reaction to people she doesn't know well is a sign that her development is right on track, not that anything is wrong with her. She is in a phase called "stranger anxiety."

Stranger anxiety is a developmental milestone that occurs at about eight months of age when babies are sufficiently mature that they know that their parents and other important adults are the source of their greatest happiness. When they see a face that is different than the one they are expecting, babies feel a loss of the pleasure they feel with their "special" people. As a result, they don't smile and they often cry. Your daughter's unhappiness with strangers in the elevator is actually the culmination of a series of accomplishments: she can distinguish her special people from others; she knows they make her the happiest, and when she sees a strange face, she knows it is not one of the faces that causes her joy. Next time your daughter looks somber or cries when she sees someone she doesn't know, smile and tell the stranger, "Believe it or not, it's a real achievement that she feels unhappy when she sees you." You can expect stranger anxiety to occur on and off for the next few months and then to be replaced with the next developmental milestone, separation anxiety.

Behavior change nothing to worry about

Q Our ten-month-old daughter has recently exhibited a significant change in behavior. She has always been an easygoing child. But she gets extremely upset when we do routine things such as placing her on the changing table. We understand that at this age babies are trying to express their independence, but seeing her get upset about such things is confusing. Is this typical and how should we respond?

A Your daughter is becoming much more aware of the world around her and she increasingly knows what she wants and that she sometimes wants something different from what you want. If she is engaged in an activity that interests her and you pick her up to change her, she may cry because she can remember that she was doing something she didn't want to leave.

If you realize that your daughter is maturing right on schedule and not being difficult or contrary, you will be able to avoid taking her protests personally. More important, you will know that diplomacy is about to become one of your most valuable parenting strategies. For example, if your daughter is playing with a portable toy, pick up the toy along with your daughter so she won't have to stop what she is doing when you put her on the changing table. Another strategy is to set aside some special toys to give her on the changing table. Or if you are sure she will be terribly upset if you take her away from what she is doing, you can even put an old towel under her on the floor and change her there.

At this age almost every transition can be difficult, because as your daughter's cognition continues to mature, she will not be as easily distracted as she once was. By planning ahead, allowing extra time and approaching changes diplomatically, you will help your daughter to navigate this delicate phase successfully and with a minimum of unhappiness.

Baby Temper Tantrums

Q My 10-month-old daughter has a terrible temper. If you try to take something from her or stop her from doing something that might hurt her, she screams until she is red in the face. But when you give in, she's fine. Is there anything I can do to try to stop this?

A We know how upsetting it is to be faced with a baby who screams hysterically when she can't have what she wants, but you will probably find it easier to give her the help she needs if you don't think of her as having a "temper." All babies and young children derive a major part of their happiness and sense of worth from getting what they want. What they wish for is what they need, because having their desires satisfied shows them that they are loved and cherished. So it is understandable that for the time being your baby will become upset and cry when you frustrate her wishes.

If you don't expect too much of her too soon, she will gradually outgrow this emotional dependence on getting what she wants. You will foster her emotional development by granting her wishes as often as possible, because in this way you will help her to maintain the stable sense of competence and self-worth that is so crucial to her healthy development. At moments when your baby can't have what she wants because her wish is dangerous or impractical, you will do her a great service if you can be understanding of her distress. Comfort her until she feels better, and if possible, interest her in an alternative adventure. Your caring response to her tears will help her learn that while she cannot always have the thing she wants, she can always count on your love and kindness.

Should I potty train my 9-month-old?

Q I read recently about a trend toward potty training babies. My baby is 9 months old and I would love to do away with the diapers. But I also know that in the past, some children's problems have been attributed to being potty trained too early. The argument for training babies is that it is better for the planet. Before I try this with my son, I want to be sure I will not be hurting him. What is your view?

A There is no question that in many parts of the world there are no diapers (or diapers are too expensive), meaning many babies eliminate directly in a designated indoor or outdoor setting. However, this arrangement works not because the babies become toilet trained but because parents or other caretakers remain physically close to them and consistently watch for signs that the children need to eliminate. It is the parents who are trained—not the babies.

If you are willing to maintain this level of vigilance, you could probably dispense with diapers, but the demands on you would be severe. This is usually not possible in our culture, where children go to daycare and parents put babies in cribs or playpens. Babies cannot reliably and voluntarily indicate they need to use the potty.

The timetable for toilet-choosing, the term we prefer, is sometime between 18 months and 4 years. Every child has a different rhythm for making that choice, and it is true that prematurely pressuring children to use the toilet will negatively affect their emotional health.

What advice can you offer for car trips with a baby?

Q What is the best way to travel with an 8-month-old baby? We are going to be taking a driving trip and staying in different places every night. Our daughter is a good sleeper, but I have heard nightmare stories about kids who are up all night and keep their parents up when they have to drive the next day. I've also heard quite a few dreadful tales of car meltdowns. We would like to have a few tricks up our sleeves in advance. Thanks.

A Traveling with a baby can be enjoyable if you take into account the baby's age-appropriate needs. Try to do most of your driving at nap times. Leave plenty of time for her to get out of her car seat and be free to kick, sit or crawl. Have new toys for difficult moments. Be prepared to sing a lot of songs and play a lot of peekaboo.

To help her sleep at night, bring her crib bumpers and favorite comfort toys so her crib will look familiar. Most important, don't put yourself on such an exhausting schedule that you can't give your baby the same quality care she would get at home.

Chapter Two
Toddlers

How to respond when a young child says, 'I hate you!'

Q I hope you can help me. What should my response be to my 3½-year-old child when he yells "I don't like you!" or "I don't love you anymore!" because he has been given a time-out or is not granted something he is crying for? I try to tell him that he is hurting my feelings by saying this. However, it does not seem to stop him.

Thank you in advance!

A First, you need to rethink your approach to discipline. Time-outs are harmful to children because they teach them to isolate themselves or to turn away from loved ones who are upset or who do not agree with them.

You want to keep in mind that your child's standard for responding to relationship differences will be determined by your responses to him. Much better than time-outs is to use our loving regulation approach, in which you manage your child's behavior without isolating, depriving or punishing him.

If you pick up your child when he is upset or is in danger of harming himself, others or property, and you soothe his tears and try to help him find another enjoyable activity, he will learn that he can remain close to those he loves even when disagreements occur. This will make his friendships as a child and as an adult smoother and more pleasurable.

Second, the inner well-being of all children under four depends to a large extent on having what they want when they want it. So it is normal for your child to cry or to feel upset if he can't have something he really wants.

When your son is upset about not having something, it is crucial to show him that you understand how painful that feels and that you want to help him feel better by giving him a hug, by listening to his feelings, and by helping him find an acceptable activity that he can enjoy.

If you make these two changes in your parenting, your son will be much less likely to tell you that he hates you or doesn't love you anymore. If in the transition period he does say those things, it is important to reassure him. Tell him that he feels that way at the moment because he is upset, but that you know that underneath, he loves you, just as you continue to love him. Informing your son that he is hurting your feelings makes him feel powerful, but it is also terribly frightening. More than anything, your son needs the security of knowing that your feelings for him remain stably loving even when he feels upset and angry with you.

Handling a two-year-old who pretends to "shoot" his mom

Q I have a two-year-old son who likes to play guns. He pretends every toy he owns is a gun. I don't know where he picked it up. I don't have a TV. I thought that if I didn't play along, he would soon become bored with this game. I try to explain what each toy is so he will use it properly but he continues "shooting" me. Recently he "shot" me and said he was killing me. I am fed up with this behavior and want it to stop. Is gunplay really that horrible that he should never be able to pretend?

A The main issue here is really not guns and violence but why your son is angry with you. While two-year-olds can often become angry when their wishes are interfered with, your son seems to be unusually resentful of you. In other words, turning his toys into guns is a symptom of the problem, not the problem itself.

Usually when two-year-olds are this hostile, it is because too much is being demanded of them. Review the ways in which you relate to your son, and consider whether you show him and tell him regularly how much you love and admire him. Perhaps you expect more in the way of socialization than is appropriate for his age and then are disapproving or punitive if he can't live up to your standards.

We are convinced that once your son feels more loved and cared for, he will respond by being more affectionate and less hostile toward you. He will then be much less attracted to play in which he turns his toys into guns and "shoots" you.

In the meantime, rather than telling him not to pretend his toys are guns, show your son that you recognize that he is angry and that you are not devastated by those feelings. If he pretends to shoot you, you might say, "I can see you are angry. Can you tell my why? I love you and would like to help you feel happier." If he continues the aggressive play, suggest another activity you know he likes and see if he will engage with you in a more positive way. But it is crucial that you don't shame or disapprove of him when he is making his toys into guns or is overcome by his negative feelings toward you. Negativity on your part will only increase the aggressive behavior you are trying to help your son leave behind.

"I hate you Mommy."

Q My three-year-old daughter has been telling me "I hate you" practically every day for the past several months. Sometimes she says it in frustration, but sometimes just in passing, which is kind of unnerving. She doesn't treat her father this way. I have responded in virtually every way I can imagine, from shrugging it off to explaining that it is hurtful. Nothing I do has any impact. How do you suggest I respond?

A The reason that your daughter is negative toward you but not toward her father is that, like all children her age, she is experiencing the turbulence of the Romantic Phase. Some time around three, it dawns on children that their parents have a special relationship from which they are excluded. They respond by seeking to get for themselves the romantic attention they see the opposite-sex parent give the same-sex parent. When they discover that they cannot win the opposite-sex parent's romantic interest away from the same-sex parent, they conclude that the same-sex parent is standing in their way and become angry. This conviction that you are thwarting her romantic wishes toward her father is the reason that your daughter says she hates you.

Once you realize that your daughter is going through a universal, normal, and temporary phase, you may find it easier to take her statements in stride. The more relaxed you can be when she tells you she hates you, the better it will be for her. Rather than shrugging off the negative remark or telling her that you are hurt by it, try to respond positively. For example, say, "I know you feel angry sometimes, but I love you and will always love you no matter what." This reassuring response is important for your daughter's development, because, deep down, she fears that her anger at you will cause you to reject her or, even, to retaliate. Your reassurance helps your daughter to realize that the drama of love and rejection is taking place only in her mind and not in reality. This realization will gradually enable her to accept that she is never going to take your place with her father, but that she will always have both of you to care for and about her.

Why won't my child's "Why's" end?

Q My 3½-year-old daughter is mired in the "why" stage and my husband and I are losing our minds. She will ask why Daddy has to go to work. We explain, but she again asks, "Why?"

After we give her a further explanation, she continues to repeat "Why?" Finally, in spite of our best intentions, we get irritated and call a time-out to questions. Then she gets upset and asks us every other second whether the time-out is up and she can ask questions again. We feel she is dragging us down to her level, but we don't know what to do. Suggestions?

A The "why" stage, like the "no" stage, can be stressful for parents, but it is perfectly normal and, if it is not turned into a power struggle, it is time-limited. In part, three-year-olds are developing a real curiosity about the world and how it works and are really interested in having their questions answered. Partly, though, they are old enough to perceive that adults seem to have a lot of fun talking to each other and that they would like to be just like Mommy and Daddy and be right at the center of ongoing conversations.

Asking "why" is a sure way to engage adults in discussion and to feel that they can have the same kind of fun that Mommy and Daddy have. It is also a way to express age-appropriate needs for attention or to handle feeling hungry, tired, or generally out of sorts. The "why" phase tapers off when children become able to engage in more sophisticated forms of dialogue and when they become more able to enjoy independent projects and play.

When your daughter asks "why," it is important not to become irritated because she will get the message that her curiosity and wish for knowledge are somehow wrong. Rather, answer a few of her questions and then gently steer her in a different direction (for example, offer food if you think she is hungry, or suggest she sit in your lap and hear a story if you think she is tired). This will allow you to escape from the "why" loop without dimming your daughter's enthusiasm for learning.

How should I deal with my toddler's endless string of "No's"?

Q My 15-month-old daughter says "no" very adamantly to almost everything I say. My healthcare provider suggested that I just ignore her or say something like "I love you" each time she says no. This isn't working. What do you recommend?

A Actually, you don't want to stop your toddler from saying "no," because her behavior is normal and necessary for her age. Your toddler's "no's" both express her age-appropriate belief in her power to control everything and everyone, and also enable her to buffer the loss all toddlers feel when they don't get what they want when they want it.

Your child will outgrow her attachment to the word "no" by herself. In the meantime, try to avoid confrontation by going underneath her radar. For example, instead of saying, "Lunch is ready," try giving her a choice. Ask, "Do you want milk or orange juice with your lunch?" Or, "Do you want Winnie the Pooh plate or the Lion King plate?"

Inevitably, you will have to make your child do something she says "no" to (getting in a car seat, taking medicine). When this happens, try to keep the discussion short ("I know you don't want to, but you need to"), get the unpleasantness over with, soothe your child, and help her move on to happier things. Remember, this too will pass.

Mom wants to know when 'No' should be used to keep kids safe.

Q I have read your *Smart Love* book and follow your column and I know that you don't recommend saying "No" to toddlers, but I don't know what to do when my 1½-year-old climbs on the furniture. He stands on the kitchen chairs and leans on the backs so that if we don't hold the chair he would go crashing to the floor. He bounces on his sister's bed and could fly off at any moment if we weren't standing there. He tries to walk on the arm of the couch. And on and on. When we tell him "No," he laughs. I even lost my temper once and slapped his hand, which I know wasn't right. He cried for a moment, but then went right back to what he was doing. My husband and I feel our son is completely out of control and don't know what to do next.

A The problem is that the nature of toddlers' minds is that they are unable to assess or even recognize danger. They are convinced they are all-powerful and invincible. That is why toddlers have to be constantly watched. There is no point in wasting your breath arguing or saying no to a toddler who is trying to engage in a risky behavior. If your son were mature enough to understand that he could be hurt, he wouldn't take the risks he takes. Saying "no" simply provokes him to "prove" to you that he is too powerful to be interfered with. When your son climbs on the furniture or goes to bounce on the bed, simply lift him up and find something more constructive for him to do. You will save yourself and him a lot of aggravation and you can be sure that by the time he is old enough to understand the effect that gravity can have on him, he will be more careful.

Baby proofing leads to safety and security

Q My one-year-old is beginning to walk and can reach a lot of the breakable items in the house. I have been telling him "No," but he is very determined. I usually end up yelling and slapping his hand. He cries and gets upset. I hate all this unpleasantness. I have a friend who put all the breakable things away. But if I do so, aren't I teaching my son that life will always be arranged for him? He won't be prepared for reality. What do you suggest?

A To understand what our children learn from us, we need to understand how their minds work. Your son is too young to understand that he can drop a rubber ball without breaking it, but he can't do the same to a piece of china. So when you say "No" to touching the china but then allow him to throw his ball, he is confused. All he knows is he is in danger of your disapproval, which inhibits his explorations. The result is the curiosity he will need as a student and an adult will become conflicted and inhibited. On the other hand, if you baby-proof your home, your son will know the joy of satisfying his natural curiosity with your approval and protection. Don't worry about creating a hot house atmosphere for him that will make life difficult later. If we didn't protect babies and young children, they wouldn't live to grow up.

How do I handle toddler meltdowns?

Q I understand and agree with your approach to toddlers—to babyproof the environment so they can explore without interference. But whenever my 14-month-old daughter gets tired or cranky and I pick her up, she pulls my ears, yanks my hair, hits me in the face and even bites. Most of the time she is very loving, but the moment she is melting down and I have to pick her up, she starts after me. I try holding her hands, but she get hysterical. I don't want to punish her, but I don't know what to do.

A You are right that this behavior needs to be managed but not punished. We call this approach "loving regulation."

Your daughter is behaving in an age-appropriate manner. When she feels tired or cranky she assumes you are the cause. Young children believe their parents are all-powerful and cause their emotions, both good and bad. Since the motivation for her aggression is the immature (but normal) assumption that you are responsible, your daughter will outgrow this. Until then, you must gently but firmly manage her reactions so she doesn't hurt you.

There are several strategies you can try. If all else fails, instead of picking her up facing you, lift her facing away from you and hold her gently under the arms until she calms down. You are showing her that you are there to help her feel better, but she won't be able to reach you. You can also carry baggies of finger food she likes, her favorite songs on a tape recorder or her favorite stuffed animal to distract her. Most important, keep in mind that this is a temporary phase.

How much unhappiness is too much unhappiness?

Q I have three children, 2 months, 3 years, and 5 years. Would you please clarify how much a child raised with *Smart Love* should cry and be unhappy. My kids are generally very happy and loving, but each of them has bad moments or bad days sometimes. At what point should I be concerned?

A The issue is not whether your children are occasionally unhappy but how you respond to their unhappiness. All babies and young children cry sometimes. Babies get hungry, overstimulated, or their tummies hurt.

Young children sometimes want to cut with real knives, cook on the real stove, take their older sister's toy, stay up past their bedtime or refuse to ride in their car seat.

Most important is not to listen to advice that tells you to isolate or ignore children who are unhappy. If you leave children to go uncomforted, they will believe that you want them to feel badly.

Because they want to feel the way they believe you want them to feel, they will develop needs to feel bad and they will also grow up believing that they should not help others who are upset.

On the other hand, if you always do your best to comfort your children when they are unhappy, they will learn that you always want to help them to feel better and they will grow up able to soothe themselves.

They also will copy you and will be caring toward others who are upset or in need of help. So ignore all advice that tells you to isolate or otherwise discipline your children when they are unhappy. Show them the love and caring that your heart tells you to provide.

Can you help me navigate birthday party minefields?

Q My son is about to have his second birthday and we have arranged a party for five friends and their parents. I have tried to plan a party he will like, but I am worried about the time he opens presents. At other birthday parties we have attended, the birthday boy tears through wrapping paper until he uncovers the present, at which point he moves on to the next gift.

The parents often try to make the child say thanks and show appreciation, but it usually doesn't happen and a power struggle ensues. Then the other kids start to move in to play with the birthday boy's presents and the child melts down completely. I don't want my son to experience this kind of unhappiness on his birthday. We would really appreciate suggestions.

A We agree that it is common but sad to see two-year-olds so unhappy at their own birthday parties. Fortunately, the problem is easily solved.

Two-year-olds are much too young to open presents neatly, admire each gift and thank the giver. Demanding this behavior from young children makes them miserable without teaching politeness.

So when guests arrive, collect the birthday presents and put them away. Your son and his friends will be free to enjoy the birthday activities. When everyone has gone home, let your son open his presents. If he prefers to tear through all the wrappings until he sees what is inside every box, you will be able to enjoy his fun without worrying about anyone else's feelings. Send thank-you's to the present-givers that include a mark or picture drawn by your son.

My 18-month-old's bite is worse than my bark

Q My 18-month-old son has been biting other children and me. I have explained over and over that biting is not acceptable and that it hurts and upsets people, but it doesn't seem to help. He does it mainly when he feels frustrated, upset or tired but I keep telling him there are better ways to handle his feelings. One of my friends suggested biting him back, but that seems to me to be stooping to his level. Suggestions?

A You are right to feel that it is not a good remedy to bite your 18-month-old. In fact, he would be likely to copy your example and bite more frequently. Similarly, explaining he is hurting others' feelings is unlikely to be effective, because at his age children's thinking is not sophisticated enough to allow them to understand how they affect the feelings of others. Best is to manage the behavior. If he is in a situation with other children, remain by his side and scoop him up if he starts to bite. Tell him in a kind but firm voice that biting is not OK and that you and he will do something else until he is ready to play without biting. The goal is not to punish him but simply to prevent him from biting. Similarly, if you can see that he is getting ready to bite you, pick him up, turn him around and hold him so he can't reach you. Tell him that you can't let him bite you, but you will be happy to play with him when he is ready. Also, consider whether your son is under undue stress in his daily life. Does he have older siblings who are pushing him around, is he spending too much time with other children? Perhaps without realizing it, you are expecting him to behave more maturely than is age appropriate. If you can remove some of the stress, you may find the biting will disappear.

Focus on crying child—not irritated bystanders

Q I am very comfortable dealing with my 2 ½-year-old child when she throws a fit at home, I am able to use your *Smart Love* approach and hold her or, if she doesn't want to be held, stick with her until she feels better.

The problem is when I am out in public. When she melts down in the grocery story, the dry cleaners, a hotel lobby or a restaurant, I feel embarrassed and my focus changes to trying to shut her down. I know this isn't ideal, but I find it hard to think of her when I know she is bothering other people. Can you help with this dilemma?

A We've all been there. It can be difficult to focus on comforting your child when the general public is giving you looks that say, "can't you shut that kid up?" It may help to keep in mind that, regardless of what others may think, your daughter is acting like a normal 2-year-old. Namely, once in a while, she gets upset and cries.

So try to use the same positive responses you would choose at home. Since you find yourself being made uncomfortable by others, the best solution may be to take her somewhere private—try going outside or into a deserted hallway, for example—and then focus on soothing her.

If you are someplace you can't leave, such as waiting in the checkout line, try turning your back to people so you can't see their expressions when you comfort your child. The idea is to create as much private space as possible to give your daughter the soothing she needs.

Uncomfortable onlooker

Q This is a question about how, as parents, we can and should react to the way other parents are treating their children. Too often I am in the grocery store and see a parent yell at or even slap their child. It pains me and I want to say something, but I don't want to make anything worse for the child by making the parent angrier.

Any suggestions how parents can say the right thing in a situation like this and help encourage angry parents not to treat their kids this way? Or is there no point and we just have to learn to turn away?

Thank you.

A This is a tough and, unfortunately, all too common situation. If the parent is clearly emotionally or physically abusive, you should find the nearest policeman or call 911 or the DCFS abuse hotline. If, on the other hand, the parent is behaving harshly without crossing the line into abusiveness, there is probably not much you can do. If you comment on the parent's behavior, you may make the parent angrier at the child and cause the parent to be even more cruel to the child when they are alone.

This is why it is so crucial that both expectant parents and new parents be helped to understand how vulnerable their children are to their anger and disapproval, and be given constructive ways to manage any anger they may experience in their children's presence.

Tears when parents go out

Q My two-year-old daughter hates it when my husband and I go out for the evening and leave her with a babysitter. I think part of the problem may be that we haven't done enough of this, but now when we try (once every two months, at the most) she clings to us and cries at the door. When I call, the sitter says that she calmed down in a few minutes and was fine, but she makes me feel so awful when we're trying to leave that I don't even want to go out any more. My husband feels like we have to go out together or we never get a chance to connect as a couple. This is starting to become an issue between us! Am I overreacting to my daughter's distress, or should we avoid putting her through this?

A One of the hardest moments for every parent is the experience of trying to leave the house with a young child clinging to you as though her heart would break. Even though your child is behaving quite normally for her age—she loves being with you and hates to see you leave—you and your husband do need an occasional night out together.

We can suggest some strategies that will make your leaving easier for your daughter to bear. First, have the babysitter come half an hour before you leave in order to involve your daughter in a special project that she really enjoys, such as making play dough, painting, reading or watching a video. If your daughter is happily engaged when it's time for you to go, she will have an easier time accepting your departure. Second, try to coordinate your outings in a way that fits well with your daughter's schedule. If she is especially tired and cranky after 6:00 p.m., try to leave for your evening out by five. If she goes to bed by 7:00 p.m., you could leave at 7:15 p.m., after she is tucked away for the night.

Sometimes even very young children can accept your departure more easily if you tell them you will phone them and say "hello" while you are gone. But if all strategies fail and your daughter cries when you leave, reassure her that you are leaving her in good hands, tell her that you understand that she hates to see you go and that you will miss her too, give her a last hug, and enjoy your time with your husband.

Loss of a father

Q My husband passed away in May. My children miss him terribly (my daughter is six and my son is 3½) and often cry. My daughter tells me she often speaks to him in her dreams and sees him while we are walking. Is this her way of mourning, or should I see a psychotherapist aside from her counseling, which she attends one time per week?

A At the moment, your daughter seems to be handling the loss as well as can be expected. She seems to have accepted the tragic fact of her father's death and to be mourning it in an age-appropriate manner. These vivid moments of re-experiencing her father may persist for many more months and, even, years, and they will fade only gradually.

One indication that your daughter is working hard to face this painful reality is that she talks with her father only in her dreams, and does not think he is really present in her waking life. Dreams are times when we rewrite reality the way we want it to be. No wonder your daughter dreams her father is back with her again! It is also not surprising that your daughter believes she catches glimpses of her father. Adults as well as children have the experience of thinking that they see an absent loved one in a crowd.

The good news is that your daughter is sharing her mourning process with you, thereby giving you a wonderful opportunity to help her grieve. Young children believe they are all-powerful, and your daughter may feel that she did something to make her father want to leave. Times when she tells you she dreams about him or sees him are golden chances to emphasize that her daddy did not want to abandon her and that sometimes even parents can't make things turn out as they want.

We know you must be struggling with your own feelings of grief just as your daughter is struggling with hers. Do share with her how much you miss her father and your knowledge that it will take a long time for that pain to ease. The strong bond you have with your children will help all of you to get through this painful and difficult process.

♥

Time-outs and other disciplines are power tools

Q I understand that spanking children is bad because it teaches them it is OK to inflict physical pain on others. But I really don't understand why you say that other disciplinary responses when children do something wrong, such as time-outs or taking away privileges like talking on the phone, are not OK. These responses do seem to work and I can't see they are harming my children. Could you please explain your position?

A Don't forget discipline works only because we are bigger and stronger and because we control the resources they need. Given that the ultimate basis for our ability to manage our children's behavior is power, and given all children copy the way their parents treat them, how we use the power we have will shape the way our children treat themselves and how they treat others. Time-outs and consequences are emotionally harsh even though they are not physically violent. When children copy these strategies for handling differences of opinion, they may become adults who withdraw from relationships when the other disagrees with them or who use money or other material goods in controlling, punitive ways. This is why we advocate loving regulation as a way of managing children's behavior. In loving regulation, the parent steps in and regulates the behavior without ever adding unpleasant consequences such as time-outs. Loving regulation is nonviolent parenting; in this increasingly violent world, we need to raise our children to be adults who can tolerate others' differences without resorting to violence-physical or emotional.

Divorced children shouldn't choose sides

Q I recently went through a bitter divorce, which I asked for and my ex-husband did not want. When my children, ages three and five, spend time with their father he says very nasty things about me. When my children come home, they are angry with me and keep asking why I won't let Daddy come back. I feel like telling them their father's whining and childish behavior is why I wanted to be rid of him, but I don't think that would be good. Is there something I can say that will make them take his side less completely and feel closer to me?

A The most important gift divorcing parents can give children is to shelter them. Children need to feel positively about both parents. Talk with your ex privately. Explain that such negative things create a contest of loyalties in which the children feel they have to choose between parents. You can also help your children understand your choice in a way that doesn't belittle their dad. For example, you could say that you just couldn't stay married to their father because the relationship wasn't good for either of you but that he still is a good dad to them and that they should continue to love him. Tell them it's OK if they wish he still lived with you. Tell them you know the divorce has been hard. But one day Dad will get over this unhappiness and realize the divorce was good for him as well.

It is important to emphasize that parents never divorce children and no matter what, you and your ex will always be their mom and dad.

65

Help us stop coat tantrums

Q It's starting to get cold now, and my thirteen-month-old who has been running around happily in next to nothing all summer, has a fit when I try to put a jacket on him. He wriggles, runs away, screams and cries. When I hold him, he tries to hit me and kick me. Usually I give in and let him go to the playground without his jacket, but then I worry he will catch cold. I don't know what I will do when winter comes. Please help.

A This is one of those tough situations that require parents to have the skills of a career diplomat. Your son needs his jacket to play outside on cold days, so letting him go out without it is not an option. Your son is not old enough to decide that for himself, but you can do everything possible to make getting it on as pleasant as possible. Here are some suggestions: Wait until you get outside. Often when young children feel the cold and the excitement of the outside world, they hardly notice when their jackets are slipped on. Give him a jacket to put on a favorite bear, then suggest he might want to look like his "friend." Or let him help you on with your jacket, which may make him more willing to let you help him into his. Hand him a box of raisins or other finger food and hope that he will be so absorbed in eating that putting on his jacket won't seem like such a burden. Get Dad or big sister to make funny noises or faces while the jacket goes on. If all else fails, you may have to hold him gently but firmly while he cries and you get the jacket on. Then do your best to comfort him.

Dressing for the weather

Q This may sound silly, but my kids, who are three, five and six, won't wear their coats. Even on cold days. Even when it's raining. Some days I insist. Other days I just say, "Okay. You can be cold (or wet) and see if that's what you want." I'm sort of inconsistent. When I insist that they wear their coats (which seems like my job, as their mother) they end up complaining a lot and it's really unpleasant. Often they take them off anyway and I have to decide how to deal with that. When I don't they are more pleasant to be with but I worry about them getting sick. What should I do?

A First, make sure they really need the coats. There is an old adage, "A sweater is something you put on when your mother is cold." So if your children don't want to put coats on or if they take them off after a few minutes, ask yourself if it is possible that they will be fine without them.

Even when the weather calls for a coat, it is often a good strategy to wait and see if your children feel chilly enough to ask for the coat themselves. The immaturity of their minds often leads children to conclude that if they are warm inside the house, they will feel warm outside too – they resist donning clothes they don't feel the need for in the house. But once they encounter a chilly blast of wind children will usually put on a jacket if it hasn't become the object of a battle of wills. Even if you have to insist, the request will seem more reasonable to the child when you are both outdoors.

Certainly, there are some instances (it is twenty-five degrees and pouring rain, it is five degrees above zero) that pose a health risk if children are unprotected even for a short time. In those instances, calmly but firmly insist that the children put their coats on before going out and that they keep them on once they are outside.

In other words, before you force the issue, make sure that your children really need protection from the cold and that they have been given every opportunity to make a sensible choice. In that case, get their coats on, chalk up their complaining to their immaturity, and try to help them move on and enjoy the rest of their day.

Should I force my son to wear boots?

Q My 2-year-old son refuses to wear boots. I don't care so much when it's raining in the summer, but in the winter when it's really cold, I don't think it's good for him to have wet feet for hours. But if I insist he put on his boots, he throws himself on the floor, kicking and screaming. We are at an impasse. What should I do?

A For health and safety reasons, you need to protect your son from his immaturity. Just as you don't start the car if he is not in his car seat, when it's cold and wet out, he needs to wear his boots so his feet stay dry. Explain to him that if he wants to play outside and walk in puddles when it is cold, he must wear his boots to stay healthy. If he says "no," bring his boots outside with you. His desire to walk in puddles may be great enough that he will put his boots on.

Once outside, you can also point out that all the other children are wearing boots—that can be a persuasive argument with 2-year-olds. If he still won't put his boots on, think of something fun to do where it is dry, such as going to a museum. If he melts down, pick him up gently but firmly, try to comfort him and direct his attention elsewhere.

Terrified of thunderstorms

Q Our almost-three-year-old is afraid of thunder and lightning. Whenever it rains, she becomes very anxious and unable to concentrate. At the first hint of thunder or lightning she covers her ears and starts screaming and crying. We have to hold her until the storm passes.

My friends say that she is just trying to get attention and that we are making the problem worse by giving in to her fears. Yet she really seems frightened. Please advise.

A Your instincts are right on! If your daughter seems frightened, she is frightened. Contrary to what you are being told, children are absolutely incapable of pretending to be miserable or terrified. In that respect, they are like all of us. If they cry, they are unhappy. So go on comforting her just as you are doing.

In addition, we suggest that you try to get at the underlying cause of your daughter's fear of storms. When children are afraid of thunder and lightning, the usual reason is that they have developed a fear of anger—either their own or someone else's. Ask yourself if your child is frequently exposed to angry emotions. If so, see what you can do to make her everyday experience calmer and more pleasant. Also consider whether your child is being punished or disapproved of when she is angry. If she has concluded that her angry feelings are unacceptable and dangerous, she may be experiencing the crashing and flashing of the thunder and lightning as angry and, therefore, as dangerous.

Try explaining to your daughter that children frequently are scared of thunder and lightning because the light and noise remind them of strong feelings that frighten them. You might ask her if she sometimes has feelings that worry her and, if so, if she would like to tell you about them.

Sometimes it helps to read age-appropriate science books that explain the dynamics of stormy weather, such as the Magic School Bus series. If none of this helps, though, you will nourish your daughter's emotional well-being if you continue to comfort her when she is upset. Eventually she will outgrow her fear of storms, but she will never forget the loving support you gave her when she was terrified.

Fear of swimming

Q This winter I tried to give my two-year-old swimming lessons, but he hated them. Every time the teacher tried to get him near the water, he started screaming and crying. I let him stop the lessons, although my husband thought that if we made him go in once he would see it wasn't so bad and would get over his fear.

Now that summer is coming and his friends will be going to the beach I want to know how to get him to go in the water. My husband again is insisting that I make him go in and get it over with, but I don't know if that will hurt him emotionally. Please advise.

A In thinking about the issue of learning to swim, it is helpful to divide your son's activities into those he must do and those that are elective. Your son must wear his seat belt, take his medicine, get enough sleep, and have a bath once in a while. There is absolutely no reason why he should learn to swim if he doesn't want to.

Sometimes parents are told that it is important to teach very young children to swim so that if they fall into water they won't drown. But the only sure way to keep children from drowning is never to let them near water unaccompanied by an adult. No responsible parent would assume that a two-year-old who knew how to swim would use that skill if he suddenly found himself in the water.

The other reason not to force your son into the water is that it will interfere with his emotional development. Imagine how upset you would feel if you confided to a friend that you were terrified of heights and she responded by dragging you out onto her 40th floor balcony. Yet parents are often advised to ignore children's fears as though they weren't sincerely felt or weren't important.

Your son will grow up to treat himself and others the way you treat him. If you are respectful of his fears and are willing to wait until he makes the choice to learn to swim, you teach him compassion for himself and others. If you pull him into the water regardless of how he feels, you unintentionally give him a model of ignoring others' feelings and using superior force to make them do as you wish. So follow your excellent instincts. Do take your son to the beach this summer, but bring lots of sand toys and make it clear to him that he doesn't have to go near the water until he wants to.

How do I convince my son monsters don't exist?

Q What do you say to a 2-year-old who says he is afraid to go to bed and open his closet because there are monsters that are going to eat him? My son first heard about monsters from his older brother, who wanted to tease and upset him, and it worked. Now he won't sleep in his room unless we sit with him. And he makes me take his clothes out of the closet for him. We have tried shining flashlights under the bed and in the closet to show him nothing is there, but he says monsters can be invisible. This behavior is making me crazy. I don't know what to do to help him. Suggestions?

A Once 2-year-olds get it in their heads something scary could happen, it can be very hard to convince them otherwise. Logical explanations usually don't work because 2-year-olds don't have the cognitive maturity to distinguish between fantasy and reality. One approach is to tell your son that his older brother was just teasing him and that monsters don't really exist. It would help if his brother would tell him that also. If your son hears his brother made up the monsters, he may feel less convinced about their reality. You can also read your son books that raise the question of monsters and then dispel kids' fears in an entertaining way, such as *The Monster at the End of This Book* by Jon Stone.

Sometimes it helps to talk to kids about how monsters represent their own feelings and do not really exist. Children are often intrigued with the notion that since monsters are made up of their feelings, the kids can be in control of the monsters and make them be friendly instead of angry.

If none of these strategies works, go along with his requests to get his clothes and sit with him while he goes to bed. Over time, his increasing maturity and your calmness will convince him he has nothing to fear.

How can I deal with my child's everyday fears?

Q My two-year-old is deathly frightened of escalators and public restrooms. He completely melts down and clings to me like plastic wrap. It's really a problem for me because sometimes I do have to go to the bathroom when we are out and my son gets totally hysterical and makes it impossible. I have talked to him about how escalators and public bathrooms can't possibly hurt him and told him that I will have to leave him home with a babysitter if he can't get over this, but he doesn't seem to be getting better. What do you suggest?

A Two-year-olds do sometimes develop irrational fears of everyday things. They get over these fears most quickly if parents remain both reassuring and accepting. It's fine to explain to your son why escalators and public bathrooms can't hurt him, but when his fears do not diminish, hug him and comfort him. It is also important to emphasize in a positive manner that someday he will feel more confident, but that, until that time, you will try to shield him from experiences that scare him. When possible, take a friend or other family member shopping with you so that someone can remain with your son if you need to use a public restroom. It's almost always possible to avoid escalators by taking stairs or elevators. Trying to force him to confront and conquer his fears will only lead to a power struggle that will prolong the time it takes for him to get over them and make him feel alienated and misunderstood. On the other hand, your patience and understanding will not only help your son to become less fearful, but will also bring the two of you closer together.

Skittish two-year-old needs comfort

Q I am having a problem with my two-year-old and I don't know what to do. He is scared of loud noises. When we are outside and there is a big machine, a fire engine or even loud traffic noises, he starts to cry and clings to me. I explain what causes the noises and that these things can't hurt him, but it doesn't seem to do any good. My husband tells him to stop acting like a baby, but he only clings to me harder. It's getting to the point that he doesn't want to go outside anymore. What do you advise?

A First recognize that when your two-year-old appears terrified, he is terrified. Children do not fake fright and unhappiness. So don't hesitate to comfort him as you would if he had skinned a knee or broken a toy. If he feels he can take refuge in the security of your arms when he is frightened, the fear will seem much less overwhelming. Refusing comfort only increases his fear by forcing him to cope with it alone. In addition, shaming your son by calling him a "baby" only adds shame to the pain he already is experiencing.

The answer to why loud noises are so frightening to your son may lie in his everyday experience. Often young children are frightened by noise when there is fighting, yelling or unusual tension in their home life or at daycare or preschool. The noise of family conflict gets generalized to other loud noises. Children who are made to feel their anger is unacceptable may become frightened of anger. They equate loud noises with anger and feel overwhelmed. Help your son become comfortable with any angry feelings he may have and, as much as possible, reduce the conflict he experiences in his world.

Nutritional worries

Q How can I make sure my 2½-year-old picky eater is getting enough nutrients?

A You can relieve a lot of your worries by giving your child a vitamin every day. Buy small quantities of children's vitamins until you find a brand he thinks tastes yummy. Then make sure that you are not pressuring your child to eat specific foods at specific times. Getting into a power struggle over eating is a lose-lose proposition. You cannot force a child to eat, and your son will get so invested in resisting that he will begin to refuse even food that he likes.

Keep in mind that two-year-olds are rarely hungry on adult timetables. As long as you are giving your son nutritious food, it really doesn't matter what time of day he eats it. Offer snacks that are healthy and fun so that if your son fills up on them, he will still get the nutrition he needs. Some of our children's favorites were carrots or celery dipped in peanut butter, black olives, frozen peas, bananas, and sliced meats with ketchup for dipping.

If you run out of ideas, there are excellent books that offer creative yet simple ideas for interesting young children in good food. And don't worry if your child skips a food group here and there. If you don't struggle over it, his body will tell him to make up for lost time in the next day or two.

Most important, try to avoid the pitfall of taking personally your child's refusal to eat food you have prepared. He is not trying to torture you. Rather, he has the determination of all two-year-olds in combination with his own individual tastes. By consulting him, offering him a selection, and not insisting on a time or place for eating, you will revive his naturally healthy appetite.

Don't have food fights with your child

Q My 2½-year-old used to be a good eater. Now, though, he only wants to eat bread, butter and jelly. I thought it was a phase, but it's been going on now for three months and I don't see an end in sight. I have tried telling him he can't have his butter and jelly sandwich until he eats some meat and vegetables, but he throws a complete tantrum and doesn't eat anything. Some days it seems like all we ever talk or think about is what he is eating. I am at my wit's end. Please advise.

A The first step is to consult your pediatrician and find out what foods besides jelly sandwiches, vitamins and milk your son needs to eat to stay healthy. Then take your son to the pediatrician and let him hear the doctor tell him what additional foods he needs every day.

Choose one meal, and make sure your son eats the added foods before he gets his jelly sandwich. If he cries, wait him out without becoming angry or isolating him. Eventually, he will be hungry enough to eat the necessary food and move on to his favorite dish. The point is you are not arguing with your child over food preferences, you are only using the same principle as when you give him medicine or put him in his car seat, namely that there are certain things that have to happen to keep him safe and those are not negotiable.

In general, it is pointless to go to war with any child, especially a two-year-old, over food preferences. If you begin using punishments or rewards for eating, you open a door you don't want to go through because you will be stuck with the consequences for years to come—hardly a meal will go by without your having to use threats or rewards to get your child to eat.

So remain firm, consistent and caring. Within the limits of preserving his health, let him eat bread, butter and jelly to his heart's content. At some point, he will outgrow this food fad and move on—and he will outgrow it sooner rather than later if you can avoid making a power struggle out of it.

Do two-year-olds need friends?

Q My two-year-old daughter has been in daycare since she was six months old. My mother just moved to the area and is willing and able to care for her. My mother is very loving and my daughter is crazy about her. But I worry about the effect of taking my daughter away from her friends at daycare and putting her in a situation where she won't see much of other children. Will this keep her from developing proper social skills?

A You highlight an issue that concerns many parents of two-year-olds; how important are friendships at this age? The answer is that friends are not nearly as important to two-year-olds as the significant adults in their lives, and, most of the time, are not even as important as their favorite toys.

Two-year-olds are in a temporary and normal stage of wanting what they want when they want it, which can make the give-and-take of a friendship periodically unappealing. Not until some time after your daughter turns three will she be ready for the generosity and mutuality necessary for real friendship.

Right now the most important influences on your daughter's feelings about herself and the world are the significant adults in her life. A positive, stable relationship with her grandmother will be a powerful force in creating and maintaining your daughter's feelings of optimism and self-worth. These qualities will provide the best platform for your daughter's friendships later on.

Feeling bored at home

Q I am a stay-at-home mom who often finds herself bored and frustrated and feels quite guilty about this feeling. I used to work, but never had a real career that mattered to me, which is why I chose to stay home instead of arranging childcare for my daughter. I love my daughter and I do think it's good that I'm home with her. But even though we go to play groups and playgrounds and museums and anything else I can think of, I feel kind of envious of working mothers who have challenging careers as well as being mothers. Is this just par for the course of raising a little kid or is there something about this that I'm missing?

A The main reason that you often feel "bored and frustrated" staying home is probably that, like many parents, you find it difficult to know what is going on in your young child's mind. When young children seem opaque to us, the daily chores of caring for them can feel repetitive and frustrating.

Even though the young child cannot express her thoughts and feelings in adult conversation, you can become attuned to her communications and know what is really transpiring in her mind. For example, making the umpteenth peanut-butter-and-jelly sandwich for the week will be more rewarding if you are aware that you are satisfying not only your daughter's hunger, but her emotional need to feel cared for by you. That feeling of being cared for will translate into the ability to grow up to be a person who cares for herself and others.

We recommend that you read books, such as our *Smart Love,* that will tell you what your child is feeling and thinking at different ages and will show you that the most ordinary daily interactions have a powerful impact on your daughter's development.

In addition, you may be missing the intellectual stimulation of interacting with other adults. If you join a book club, take a continuing education course, or make an effort to have lunch or dinner with friends on a regular basis, you will feel less confined and more able to enjoy your time with your daughter.

Trying to keep our child from being selfish.

Q I read your column and bought a copy of your book, *Smart Love*. Your ideas seem very kind and caring, but I worry that if they are applied in the real world, children will end up egocentric and spoiled, thinking they should always get their way. I was always taught "Others first, myself second," and I have to think that is the way to raise good people. I would be very interested in your response, because otherwise, I think your approach is very appealing.

A In reality, the *Smart Love* approach to child-rearing should produce children who are especially generous and compassionate and not at all egocentric or "spoiled." Because children learn by imitation, kind, caring responses that are tailored to a child's developmental stage teach children kindness and compassion toward themselves and others.

Trying to force children to share or to be altruistic before they are old enough to choose those virtues for themselves causes resentment and teaches coercion as a model for making others do as you want. Moreover, our approach does not amount to permissiveness. Permissiveness can produce children who behave in ways adults term "spoiled" because this approach amounts to the absence of the kind of help and guidance children need.

Children of permissive parents are unable to tolerate frustration and, consequently, can be out of control. In contrast, *Smart Love* principles offer parents an effective way to manage children's behavior in an age-appropriate and loving manner. So follow your instincts to love and enjoy your children. In doing so, you will help them, not harm them.

Must my toddler say please?

Q Our 3-year-old really resists saying "please" and "thank you." We have tried everything from insisting he can't have whatever it is until he says please and thank you to trying to make a game of it.

My husband thinks this is much more important than I do. When other people give my son little gifts, my husband won't allow him to accept it until he says thank you. At home he won't give him anything unless he says please first. I feel my son is still young and there is plenty of time for him to learn manners.

This is becoming a real disagreement between my husband and myself. What do you think?

A True manners are learned only by imitation. If you and your husband always say "please" and "thank you" to each other, to your son and to others, your son will pick up this habit on his own in the next few years. At that point, he will feel good about these forms of politeness because using them will make him feel grown up.

Three-year-olds do not naturally say "please" and "thank you" consistently, and trying to force them is likely to cause resentment and rebellion. You can make young children imitate polite speech, but they only say the words in order to get what they want.

Your goal is to inspire your son to be polite, in which case he will want to be polite even when you are not around.

How can parents encourage children to be polite?

Q My husband and I agree that having children with good manners is important but my husband has decided that he does not want our children to say "please" for anything! He would prefer that they say more affirming statements such as, "I would like..." or "I want...," but not say, "May I please have..." or, "Can I have... please?"

I think my husband has a point, but I believe that as children they still have to ask permission for items, and as adults they will have the right to make affirming statements without having to ask permission. What do you think is the best choice to make? My children are ages four and two.

A The real problem here is your assumption about the best way to raise children to be polite, considerate adults. Forcing young children to use specific words to ask for what they want does not mean that they will continue to use these words when they are old enough to have a choice. We can always make young children behave as we want. The issue is how to make them want to behave considerately when they are not under our direct control.

The best way to do that is to treat them with politeness and respect. If you always say "please" and use an affectionate tone when you ask your children to do something, they will copy you and, over time, will grow into thoughtful, polite individuals. It is so important to keep in mind that the most formative influence on our children is not what we say or what we make our children say, but how we treat them.

How can we make our boys more gracious?

Q With the holidays coming, we are again facing the question of how to get our boys, ages 2, 4 and 6 to say appropriate thank you's for the presents they get from their relatives. Some presents come from far away and require some sort of note. Others are given to them in person. Usually, they dive into the presents and vie a perfunctory "thank you" when pressured, but I don't think the relatives who have gone to all the trouble to choose and wrap gifts feel properly appreciated. The note writing is even worse when all we hear is, "later." My husband and I feel the children are taking present-getting for granted. How do we get them to be more gracious?

A First of all, it's important to differentiate among your children in terms of age. It is too much to expect a 2-year-old to take a break from looking at a new toy to say a "proper" thank you. You can try saying, "Can you say 'thank you' to Aunt Anne?" as your 2-year-old is ripping the present from its wrapping. But if no response is forthcoming, tell Aunt Anne what a wonderful choice she made and how much your son will enjoy it. The 4- and 6-year-olds are more able to say thank you reliably, but, again, their focus will be on the present rather than on expressions of gratitude. One strategy is to wait until they have played with the new toy for a while, at which point they may have more emotional space to give heart-felt thanks. Again, if they fall a little short, fill in for them by remarking how much use they will get from the gift and what an inspired choice it was. As for the notes, we suggest that you make printed thank-you cards with each child's name on them. Then the child can "write" his name and/ or draw a picture which will seem easier and more fun than facing a blank page. The goal is not to make the child feel inadequate or criticized because he isn't old enough to engage in adult-style gratitude, but to praise him for his age-appropriate efforts.

Mom who feels ignored

Q How do I get my 3½-year-old son to listen to me? And how do I manage to control my temper when he ignores me? I usually have the toughest time with this during transitions. For example, when we are getting ready to leave the house, I will ask him about 400 times to put his shoes on. By the 400th time, when I've gotten my one-year-old daughter ready to go and in the car, my patience is pretty much exhausted with my son. He ignores me until I raise my voice, or say, "Mommy is getting very angry with you for not putting on your shoes." Then he'll sort of meander over to his shoes and tell me he can't put them on, etc., etc.

Another example is after preschool. In the car on the way home, I always ask him what he did at school, who he played with, etc., and he frequently ignores me. I used to say things like, "Mommy doesn't like it when you don't answer my questions," or "It's rude not to answer questions," which, of course, did nothing. Now I just ask questions and shut up when he doesn't answer. But I feel frustrated and angry when he ignores me. Any suggestions?

A The reasons for your feelings of being ignored in the two examples you give are quite different, and so we will discuss them separately.

In the first example, the problem is less that you are being ignored than that you are expecting too much of your three-year-old, with the result that you are frustrated when he doesn't respond as you wish. Three-year-olds normally have great difficulty with transitions and need lots of tactful help to make them peacefully. This is especially true when there is a one-year-old sister getting all the attention and assistance that the three-year-old still needs and wants.

We suggest that instead of simply telling your son to put his shoes on, you get his shoes, put him in your lap, and help him on with his shoes while you sing a song or talk about the fun he will have on the outing. If he says he wants to put his shoes on himself do praise him, but don't expect that he will want to do this himself the next time. If you take his true emotional age into account and help him now with shoes, jacket, etc., in order to make possible a calm and comfortable transition, you will not feel frustrated and ignored, your son will experience the warmth of being understood and cared for, and your relationship will immediately become closer and more enjoyable. When he does begin to do more for himself, it will be out of pleasure and a feeling of competence and not from feelings of shame or worries about your displeasure.

A lot of the frustration you describe in your second example is the result of not realizing that three-year-old children hold conversations very differently from adults. Children that age often are speechless when asked general questions such as, "What did you do today?" Moreover, if something went wrong at school they often dislike discussing the discomfort they felt. So if you ask your son who he played with and things did not go well with his friends, he may not feel like answering.

If you consider his silence as the result of immaturity rather than rudeness, you will have taken a big step toward being able to have a conversation with him that is appropriate for his age. Try asking questions that you think will allow him to relive activities he enjoyed. For example, if he likes animals, ask him how the hamsters were feeling today. Or if you know he enjoys art, ask if he worked with clay or painted a picture.

Most important, don't get angry with your son if he doesn't answer a question. When children that age don't know what to say or don't want to talk about something, they frequently remain silent. Your son is not deliberately upsetting you—he is just acting his age. When you get irritated with him for not answering, you make it more difficult for him to be outgoing and responsive. If you bring up topics that your son finds enjoyable in a relaxed and non-pressured manner, you will be amazed at how much of his day he will want to share with you.

How can I protect my overly curious toddler?

Q My 18-month-old girl is wonderfully curious and outgoing. The problem is that she has no fear. We live in an apartment building that has a lot of dog owners. When a dog is on the elevator with us (which happens all the time) she rushes over to pet it. Once or twice a dog has growled or acted unfriendly, and I am really worried she will be bitten.

I have told her over and over that not all dogs are friendly and that we need to ask the dog's owner if it's OK to pet the dog, but she gets so excited when she sees a dog that all my warnings go out the window. I hate to start punishing her, but I can't seem to get through any other way. How can I stop this behavior?

A Just as you would not expect to explain to an 18-month-old that it is dangerous to run into the street and then rely on her ability to keep herself safe from traffic, there is absolutely no good way to explain to your daughter that strange dogs can hurt her.

Children under three do not have the mental ability to grasp hypothetical statements such as, "If you go near that dog, it could bite you." Because she cannot understand future dangers, your daughter needs to be protected in a way that does not dampen her confidence and curiosity. Punishing her would confuse her and make her feel inadequate, but it would guarantee that she won't run up to the next dog she sees.

The best solution is to make sure you always have her hand or are able to scoop her up out of harms way if a dog is in the elevator. You will keep her safe without putting a damper on her age-appropriate desire to explore her world. After she is three, she will be able to understand that some dogs aren't friendly and she will want to stay safe by staying away from dogs she doesn't know.

Handling curiosity

Q I turned my back on my two-year-old to talk on the phone for one second and when I turned around she was eating the cat's food. I was so horrified that I yelled "No!!" at which point she burst into tears. I know that my reaction was too strong, but I would like to know what I should have done (a time-out, a consequence?) to teach her to stay away from the cat's food.

A It may seem surprising, but the best response would have been to pick up your daughter, give her a hug, tell her gently that the cat food is not for eating, and move on. Punishments will not teach her anything other than that you get unpredictably angry and that curiosity is dangerous.

Parents are often misadvised that they must teach their young children to avoid dangerous situations. But children your daughter's age are simply not old enough to understand that an empty street can suddenly contain a car, that a pretty flame can hurt, or that food that is good for the cat is not good for them. So when they are scolded or punished for "risky" behaviors, young children feel ashamed and bad without knowing why what they did was wrong. As a result, their confidence and curiosity can be dampened.

Much better is to keep the matches out of sight, the child away from the street, and the cat food high enough that your daughter cannot reach it. Prevention is both the best way to keep your daughter safe and also to preserve her natural optimism and curiosity. By the time your daughter is old enough to understand why she shouldn't do certain things, she will want to avoid these risky behaviors because she will want to take the same good care of herself you take of her.

Introducing a puppy to a toddler

Q I have a four-year-old son and a two-year-old daughter. My son has been begging for a puppy and I would like to get one for him. He loves animals and is very responsible. But I am worried about my daughter. We went to the house of a friend who has a dog and even though I told her repeatedly not to play with it, she kept chasing after the dog until it growled and had to be locked up. If we get a puppy, how can I teach her to leave it alone?

A You can't teach a two-year-old to leave a dog alone. You can either keep the dog locked away, make sure you are always in the room with your daughter and the dog, or wait until your daughter is at least three to get a puppy.

Even if you choose a forgiving breed, your daughter's age-appropriate immaturity may cause her to push things too far, with the result that the dog will snap at her or she will hurt the puppy in some way. If you already had a dog, you would be in for a difficult period, but since you have the option of waiting, why not get a puppy when both children are old enough to enjoy it and treat it properly.

Two-year-olds do not have minds that can understand either what can happen to them or what they can do to someone else. This is why you can't leave a two-year-old unattended next to a hot stove, a road, a baby, or a puppy. Sometimes parents are told to "teach" their two-year-old about the dangers of the street or that it is wrong to pull the cat's tail. But a two-year-old will not understand the explanation; she will only know that her beloved parents are disappointed in her for reasons she cannot understand and she may come to feel that curiosity and initiative are bad. This is why you want to manage a two-year-old's behavior lovingly by picking her up with a smile, and to the extent possible, making her environment safe for exploration.

If you treat her in this fashion, when she is old enough to understand the consequences of her actions, she will treat her puppy with the same kindness and caring she experienced with you.

Help for handling gun play

Q My almost-four-year-old son is obsessed with guns. We aren't willing to let him have toy guns, so he makes guns out of everything, from Legos to sticks. We're always telling him to stop it, but I worry that we're only making guns more desirable. How can we discourage his interest in guns?

A You are very perceptive to notice that forbidding your son's pretend play with guns is actually making this activity more desirable to him. Instead, try to approach the problem indirectly.

If you haven't already done so, eliminate all violent movies, TV shows, and video and computer games from your son's daily experience. Unfortunately, boys have many models in our culture that equate masculinity with aggression and, specifically, with firearms. The heroes in many TV programs and video games are those men who are the most proficient killers. Since, like all children, your son is a born imitator, eliminating these aggressive models and substituting non-violent heroes will reduce his fascination with guns. There are many absorbing non-violent videos, computer games, and TV shows for young children.

Next, we suggest that you consider your relationship with your child. At four, your son still needs lots of hugs and he also needs a lot of focused, positive attention. The more lovable and loved he feels, the less attractive guns will be as a form of self-expression. And if you are following popular prescriptions to use disciplinary measures, such as time-outs, restriction of privileges, or, even, spanking, then without meaning to you are teaching your son to turn to aggression to solve relationship problems. In the mind of a four-year-old, there is not a lot of difference among guns, fists, harsh words, and punishments. Much better is to be in charge of your son without disciplining him. For example, if he melts down because he can't have ice cream before dinner, there is no reason to send him to his room or scold him. If you offer him a hug and tell him he can have ice cream after he eats, he will learn that he can't always have what he wants, but he can always have a positive relationship with you. Over time, he will be less inclined to turn to gun play because he will be following your example and turning to non-aggressive ways of solving problems.

Finally, your primary goal is not to prevent your son from all pretend play with guns but to reduce his need to turn to aggressive play to feel a sense of well-being. If he increasingly chooses more positive ways to enjoy himself, the occasional pretend gun battle will not be harmful to him.

Responding to cuss words

Q How should I handle a 2½-year-old child who uses bad words? Soap in the mouth?

A The way to get a two-year-old to use "good" words is to make sure that these are the only words she hears. Your daughter's sprouting language skills rest on her ability to imitate others' speech, which she soaks up like a sponge. So if she is saying "bad" words, the reason is that she is innocently repeating words she is hearing.

A two-year-old cannot possibly comprehend the distinction

between bad words and good words. As a result, if you reprimand a two-year-old for using particular words, you only confuse her, upset her, and dent her pride in her dawning ability to learn words and put them together first into phrases and then into sentences. Moreover, because your two-year-old is too young to understand why a word is bad, she will never know whether the next word she says will be acceptable or unacceptable to you. The combination of confusion, uncertainty and self-doubt produced by disapproving of her speech will make it harder for her to learn our language.

If your two-year-old does use a word you find offensive, the best response is just to repeat her sentence and substitute a word you prefer. For example, if she says, "There goes the @&%$ cat," you can say, "Yes, there goes our pretty cat." Since imitation is the basis of her language learning, if she ceases to hear the offensive word, she will also stop saying it. On the other hand, if you focus her attention on the word by telling her not to say it, her two-year-old assertiveness will be activated and she may begin using it in every sentence.

Should I make my toddler study harder?

Q I recently read an article about programs that teach pre-preschoolers (ages 1-3) reading and math skills. The programs have the children sit at desks for 15 minutes and memorize reading words and math operations.

I know many schools expect children to enter first grade able to read and do some math and I don't want my 18-month-old left behind. At the same time, she resists attempts to get her to sit still and follow directions, and I worry that she won't have fun with this program and will dislike school before she even gets there. What is your opinion?

A Your concern is well-founded. Many studies have shown that toddlers learn best by playing with blocks or making shapes out of Play-Doh, and spending time reading or playing with loved ones. Trying to make 18-month-olds learn in ways more appropriate to older children can create negative attitudes toward learning. For example, learning formal addition and subtraction is meaningless to an 18-month-old. It would be much better to start teaching the concept of numbers by asking your daughter if she wants one grape, two grapes or three grapes.

So follow your heart and let your child learn through playing and doing and through her relationship with you. Fostering her curiosity and love of learning will stand her in much better stead as she enters school than forcing her into meaningless memorization and drills.

Give us some tips on what to look for in daycare

Q Could you write something that would help my husband and me choose a daycare environment for our 2-year-old? We both work eight hour days and we are very worried about leaving her with strangers. Between the two of us, we have been fortunate enough to be able to take parental leave time and have grandma babysit until this point, but now we have to find a place for our daughter during weekdays. Our first choice would be to hire a sitter in our home, but we cannot afford it. Besides the obvious importance that they be clean and otherwise adequate physically, what should we be looking for, from an emotional standpoint, in different daycare settings? What checklist would you recommend?

A   There are a number of things to look for in choosing a daycare setting that will foster rather than harm your child's emotional health. To ensure that your daughter gets enough attention, there should be a high ratio of staff to children, and to guarantee that the attachments she forms are not interrupted, try to find a setting with little staff turnover. Ideally, at least one or two members of the staff should have some sort of qualification in child-related areas, such as teaching or child development. Inquire about staff's attitude about children and managing their behavior. They should focus on gently helping children through difficult times and on arranging the space and the timing of activities so as to reduce conflict and increase engaged play. Watch the staff at work. You should feel that they enjoy children. Observe the children who are already there. Do they seem busy and happy? Is there a lot of conflict between children? Are older children allowed to pick on younger children? Call parents for references.

Once you choose a daycare center and enroll your child, make a surprise visit or two, and also take seriously any significant negative changes in your child's moods or behavior. These precautions and any others you can think of will make it much more likely that your child's experience at daycare will be both enjoyable and emotionally healthful.

♥

Resistance to preschool

Q   Are recurring bouts of separation anxiety common? Our three-year-old son started an all day preschool program last fall. It took him about three weeks to adjust. He was fine until after Thanksgiving, when periodic episodes of crying started. The episodes escalated until they became daily occurrences. He has even started creating reasons why he does not want to go to school, or he says he'll miss me. When I leave he is crying his heart out; I feel like I'm abandoning him. What can we do to make him feel more comfortable about school?

A You are right to be concerned about your son's persistent unhappiness at school. There are a number of possibilities to consider.

Perhaps the school is a good one for him, but he is simply not emotionally ready for the stress of being at school and apart from you all day. It is a rare three-year-old who can thrive at school for so many hours. Ask him if he would like to go for a shorter time, and if he responds positively, send him for the morning or afternoon only.

If he is still not happy, it is possible that the school or the teacher is not a good fit for him. Try observing your child's class to see if the teacher is warm and positive and the atmosphere is nurturing. If not, change teachers or visit other preschools to see if he seems happier.

Perhaps, though, he is just not ready for school this year. There are any number of three-year-olds who are not ready for school and who benefit greatly from waiting another year.

You can assess your son's readiness for school by determining: whether he is comfortable separating from you in other contexts (he will go to a friend's house to play, he likes to go with his grandfather to the park); whether he generally enjoys playing with other children; whether he can focus on a project for at least 20 minutes at a time; and whether he is generally able to follow directions.

Do remember that when your child starts school is not nearly as important as how he feels when he is there. The object of preschool is to have your child feel happy and competent, which is the best preparation for grammar school.

In other words, you are right to conclude that it is not good for your child to feel so unhappy at school and some solution needs to be found.

Should a 3-year-old be forced to go to preschool?

Q My daughter, who turned three in July, will be starting preschool in September. She says she isn't going to go. When I ask why, she says she knows she won't like it, and that it won't be fun. When I describe all of the wonderful things there will be to do, the friends she will make, and the nice teachers she will have, she says she doesn't care, she wants to stay home. My friends say to tell her she has to go. But I worry that forcing her isn't a good idea. What do you think?

A There are two possible reasons for your daughter's aversion to starting preschool. The first is that she is feeling anxious about separating from you and about committing herself to the unknown. The second is that she really is not ready for preschool and should wait a year.

To ease her fear of separating, assure her that you will stay with her at school as long as she needs you. Most preschools are now sensitive to the fact that children have different timetables for separating; some children immerse themselves in the classroom activities immediately and never look back; others need a week or two of having a parent available for comfort and refueling. To address her concerns about preschool, check to see whether the preschool has a summer program. That would allow her to see the classroom and observe the fun the children are having.

But if, despite all your efforts, your daughter remains terribly upset at the thought of going to school, there is no harm in waiting a year. With another year to mature, your daughter should enter school ready to learn and enjoy herself, and she will take that positive attitude into the later grades. Forcing her to go when she feels scared and upset may sour her on school and be the source of learning problems in future years.

Deciding whether to send a three-year-old to preschool

Q There is an increasing trend for starting three-year-olds in preschool. Is it necessary? Are there any educational gains? Will my daughter be behind if she waits another year? Thanks.

A The purpose of preschool is not to teach your child any particular content, such as color or numbers, but to introduce her to the school setting and show her that it can be enjoyable. If your three-year-old likes to play with other children, uses the potty and is comfortable separating from you for a few hours, she is probably ready for a good preschool. She will be able to enjoy it and have a positive first school experience. On the other hand, if she tends to squabble over toys, isn't potty trained or has difficulty separating from you, there is no reason to put her in a school situation. Doing so may leave her convinced that school is frightening, painful or otherwise unpleasant. There is every reason to wait a year until she is more ready.

If you conclude that your child is ready for preschool but you are a stay-at-home parent who wants another year to enjoy her full-time, don't worry about keeping her home. Missing the first year of preschool will have no educational significance for her and she will have the deep pleasure of spending her days with a parent who loves being with her. Not much is at stake either way as long as you don't send your daughter to school before she is ready. If you do enroll her, choose a preschool where the director and staff understand that its most important job is to help children feel comfortable at school rather than to socialize them or teach them anything in particular.

How should I handle my child's adjustment to preschool?

Q My three-year-old son is going to be starting preschool and the school he will be attending doesn't want parents to stay after the first day. My son is feeling somewhat nervous about starting school and I think he is going to want me to stay more than one day. The school says that my being there longer will interfere with my son's adjustment to school. But the thought of leaving him when he's unhappy doesn't feel comfortable to me. What do you think?

A We think that you have excellent instincts! Your son's preschool is making a common error when it tells you that even though your son wants you to stay with him for a while, he will make a better "adjustment" without you. The problem is that many preschools equate a child's lack of complaining or tears with a good adjustment. When parents are made to leave before a child feels comfortable, the child feels helpless and sad, which makes him become passive and appear "adjusted."

In reality, a child makes a truly good adjustment when he feels confident, cared for and full of zest for the school experience, and that is most likely to happen when he doesn't feel his parents are being ripped away from him before he is ready. If you stay until your child feels comfortable having you leave, the process may take a while. Your child may want you to stay the whole time for a few days and then to be gone only for an hour or two for another few days. Most often, within a week your child will be happy to go by himself.

If you are able to remain available to his needs and his timetable, he will associate the school experience with feeling loved, cared for and in control. This will set the tone for the many years of school to follow. Please turn a deaf ear to anyone who says that if you respond to your child's wishes for you to stay, you are being manipulated or your child will never let you go. Imagine if every time you told a loved one you needed him or her, the person accused you of being manipulative. If your child feels he needs you, he needs you, even if an outside observer believes he could do without you. Our experience is that the moment a child really feels comfortable in school, he is more than happy to play with his friends and let his parents leave. So follow your compassionate instincts and tell the preschool you are going to stay as long as your child wants you to.

💜

Fighting in front of your child

Q My husband thinks we should never fight in front of our toddler. I say it's unhealthy for our son to never see us arguing. What should we do if we're fighting?

A In this case, we must agree with your husband. Your toddler is too young to realize that you and your husband still love each other when you fight. Because he's so young, he can't understand that his parents can be angry with each other and still love him. As a result, if you argue in front of him, he will feel as if he himself is under attack and his sense of security and well-being will be badly shaken.

All parents occasionally become angry with each other in the presence of their young children, but if you manage to maintain a reasonably pleasant atmosphere until you are alone, you will spare your son from dealing with relationship complexities for which he is developmentally unprepared. However, if, in spite of your best intentions, a quarrel breaks out in front of your son, stop the hostilities as soon as you can and reassure your son by saying, "We're sorry we upset you—we know it's hard for you when we argue. Mommy and Daddy love each other even when we fight, and we both love you all the time!"

There is a popular but mistaken notion that "real life" unpleasantness will strengthen the character of the young. In reality, their developmental immaturity prevents young children from defending themselves against the emotional pain they feel when things go wrong. So parental arguments and other painful events leave young children more—rather than less—vulnerable to stress. On the other hand, if you shield your son from distressing experiences in general, and especially from the pain of witnessing you and your husband fighting, over time he will develop an abiding optimism about his world and his ability to have the harmony and love that he wants and needs. As he grows older, this positive outlook will give him the strength and resilience to respond effectively to the challenges of everyday life.

You and your husband clearly have your son's best interests at heart. So the next time you feel angry at each other in his presence, try to remember that what feels like an everyday blowup to you feels like a nuclear explosion to him, and do your best to contain your anger until you are alone. Postponing your quarrel will be easier if you realize that in this way you nourish your son's emotional well-being as surely as you care for his physical health by keeping him out of the street and away from a hot stove.

♥

Dealing with my son's behavior at the playground

Q My 3-year-old loves to explore-when we go to the playground, he takes off. Then at some point he realizes I am not right beside him, he panics and starts to cry hysterically. When I arrive he is usually surrounded by concerned parents and jumps on me as though I abandoned him, wraps his arms around me and clings like plastic wrap. I feel embarrassed and irritated by this repeated behavior. I have thought about forbidding him to leave my side, but I don't want to turn him into a mama's boy. What do you recommend?

A The best solution is to put your track shoes on and try to stay near him when he takes off. That way when he turns around, you will be right there beside him. As his panic when he can't see you shows, your son is not trying to get away from you. Rather, he has a wonderful enthusiasm and curiosity, which you are right not to want to dampen.

For moments when you are tired, try to engage him in a more stationary activity, such as building a castle in the sandbox. Or try to find fenced playgrounds with good sight lines. Most important, though, is to keep in mind both that this is a temporary phase, and also that it will do wonders for his outlook on life to know that you approve of his wishes to explore his world and are willing to provide the safety net he needs when he takes a breath and looks around.

What can I do about separation anxiety?

Q In your column last month, you discussed stranger anxiety and said that the next developmental milestone was separation anxiety. I have a thirteen-month-old daughter who is driving me crazy because she won't let me out of her sight. When I go to the bathroom, I have to leave the door open. Every time my husband and I go out, she howls and makes us feel bad about leaving. Is this separation anxiety, and what can we do about it?

A There is no question that your child is experiencing separation anxiety. Like stranger anxiety, separation anxiety is actually a result of your child's normal maturation. She knows that you are the source of her greatest happiness. Before, she was consciously aware of your absence only when she saw a strange face (stranger anxiety). Now she has the cognitive capacity to realize when you aren't there and to want you back.

As your daughter continues to mature, she eventually will know that when you leave you still exist and you will come back. At that point, she will not fall apart when you go into the bathroom and shut the door. But for now she is very vulnerable to the pain of not having you there. Rather than trying to "cure" her of her reactions, try to avoid setting them off whenever possible. The less you upset her by leaving in conspicuous ways, the sooner she will know that you really are always there for her. This inner security will one day make it possible for her to watch you shut a bathroom door or leave the house without tears or protest. So for now, try to go out with your husband after your daughter is asleep, leave doors open so she can see you (or play knocking games from the other side so she knows you are there), and don't plan extended vacations without her. Your repayment for these small sacrifices will be your daughter's unblemished optimism and happiness.

Will consoling boys make them wimps?

Q I have two sons who are 3 and 2 years old. If either one cries after being hit by the other, falling down, bumping or squeezing a body part, my husband consoles them by saying, "You're OK," and tells them to stop crying. His logic is to "toughen them up" and not raise "sissies" I believe at their ages, children should explore their emotions instead of stunting them. Is it possible that my husband's consolation technique will affect our boys' emotional development?

A You are so right. What your husband is doing is contradicting your sons' self-experience of feeling hurt and/or scared. In other words, he is telling them that it is bad to listen to themselves and shameful to cry when they feel bad. Children tend to adopt parents' attitudes toward them, and your sons will do their best to do what your husband says and ignore their feelings and avoid tears. So rather than making them tough in a good way, namely resilient and in touch with their feelings, your husband's approach will cause your sons to become tough in the sense of being out of touch with their emotions and indifferent to others' pain. They may have great difficulty being compassionate toward friends and, as adults, toward partners, and their own children.

Another danger is that, as adults, they will deny illness and injury and won't seek medical attention when necessary. You need to explain to your husband that acknowledging feelings of pain and unhappiness are signs of strength rather than of weakness-that true heroes always know how they feel and what they are risking.

If your husband won't or can't change his approach, you need to make sure they have a different example to follow. Tell your boys that you and their dad both love them but that you disagree about whether it's ok to cry and to feel upset and that you are always available to listen if they are feeling badly.

If my three-year-old doesn't try, can he build confidence?

Q My husband and I have a three-year-old boy who often says that he is no good at things. For example, when my husband asks him if he would like to play catch, he says no because he isn't any good at it. We tell him he does just fine, but it doesn't seem to affect his negative mood.

We have read that children and adults get their self-esteem from doing things well. If that's the case, my son seems stuck in a vicious circle. He doesn't try things because he thinks he can't do them. Since he doesn't try, he can't improve so he never feels better about himself. What do you advise?

A Well-being that depends on succeeding evaporates in the face of defeat. Children and adults who need to succeed to feel good about themselves tend to put too much emphasis on winning, which can make them overly competitive and poor sports.

Genuine self-esteem starts with the feelings of being lovable, loving and loved that children get from parents and other important adults. Children who receive that gift become adults with a well-being that is unaffected by success or failure.

There is a different, secondary, kind of self-esteem that children get from external success. Young children often get frustrated and their secondary self-esteem diminishes when they can't have what they want, such as someone else's toy. As they mature, children begin to develop the capacity to maintain their secondary self-esteem by making a good effort — if their team plays well but loses, they can still feel happy.

Your son is still at an age when success and failure affects his secondary self-esteem. He is trying to avoid the pain of failure by saying he is "no good" and refusing to try.

You can assist him in two ways. First, show him lots of affection, don't expect too much of him and comfort him when he is frustrated so he will develop the kind of basic self-esteem that comes from feeling cared for.

Second, volunteer to help him in areas where he feels he is "no good" and praise him for any efforts he makes. Be sure not to send the message that he has to be a "star" to make you proud. If you are consistently positive, he will be less concerned with whether he is "good" or "bad" at an activity and will focus more on enjoying himself. At that point, dropping a ball or losing a point will not be so painful, and your son will feel more like participating and less like sitting on the sidelines.

We should add that three-year-olds sometimes say "I can't" when they want their parents to do something for them (as in, "I can't get my boots on," "I can't button my shirt"). This is normal behavior they will outgrow. It is not worth worrying about.

If parents refuse, the child may be driven to prove his incompetence in order to get the assistance he wants. If you think this is sometimes the case with your son, just say affectionately, "Actually, I know you can do it yourself, but I am very happy to do it for you."

Can toddlers play nice?

Q I am writing to ask your advice about our 2½-year-old son. He is not very good at getting along with other kids. He grabs their toys and won't let them use his. When we tell him that if he won't share a toy he can't play with it either and take it away from him, he throws a fit. When we make him give back a toy, he cries. We have tried lecturing him about the importance of sharing but he just covers his ears and refuses to listen. We want to start him in preschool next September and are worried that he will be the class terror if he doesn't start behaving better now. How can we get him to be more socially appropriate?

A Ironically, the best way to make sure that your son becomes a generous, caring person is not to pressure him into sharing too early. It is so easy to forget that children's minds are very different from adults. We cannot demand behaviors from children appropriate for adults but way too advanced for a young child. You know that you couldn't put your son behind the wheel of a car or let him cross a busy street alone, yet, like many parents, you are expecting him to have the social graces of an adult.

The inner well-being of children three and under is dependent on getting what they want when they want it. This is a phase that will be outgrown naturally if there is no interference. So when a two-year-old refuses to share or grabs other children's toys, he is behaving age-appropriately, and not exhibiting personality traits to be curbed. For this reason, two-year-olds should not be asked to share. If they grab a toy and the owner wants it back, return the toy as diplomatically as possible without lectures or disapproval, and find a replacement. Understand that your son's behavior is appropriate for his age and don't force him to grow up prematurely. And sometime between the ages of three and four, he will begin to share and stop grabbing. At that age, friendships start to become more important than things and he will realize generosity and patience are important in making and keeping friends. If you let your son behave in ways that are appropriate for his age now, by the time he goes to preschool he should be ready to share and to wait his turn for toys others are using.

Who really benefits from mom-and-tot programs?

Q I have a thirteen-month-old daughter and I wonder how important it is to take her to mom-and-tot programs. I prefer taking her places with my friends, going for walks or just hanging out at the playground.

When we get together with other mothers and their kids, there is a lot of grabbing and crying and the kids don't seem to enjoy it that much. But if this kind of socializing is important for her, I am willing to participate in it.

A Most parents worry that their children need to play with other children at a very tender age. The fact is, though, that while parents often benefit from having some time to socialize with other parents, children under three do not particularly profit from playing with other children because they are still in a phase in which they care mostly about having the things they want.

Other children are tolerated and even enjoyed so long as they do exactly what the toddler wants them to do and in no way obstruct her wishes. Children under three are not mature enough to care about having "friends" or to be consistently concerned with their playmates' feelings.

Unfortunately, when parents see their young children grabbing and refusing to share, they often feel they must force them to be generous. But because children under three are too young to understand or care about others' feelings, if parents make them share they are not learning to be generous, they obey only because they are forced to or because their parents' approval is important. Underneath, though, they resent being made to give up a toy they really want and they may cling more desperately to it the next time.

If parents would just wait until the child is mature enough to realize that friends are a greater source of enjoyment than toys (usually about age four) the child will want to share in order to keep friendships running smoothly. So you do not need to worry if your child is not regularly exposed to other children her age. At this point, her parents are the most important people in her world.

What she really wants and needs is for you to notice and admire her new words, her increasing ability to do clever things with her hands and for you to follow her as she runs off to explore new territory. She is lucky that you enjoy her and love spending time with her.

♥

Forcing two-year-olds to share

Q This fall I put my two-year-old daughter in a playgroup with four other children. The problem is that the mothers don't agree about what is socially appropriate behavior. I don't want my child to be made to share, and I hate to punish her for grabbing, but two of the other mothers are adamant that these behaviors should not be allowed and the fourth mother feels confused.

Who do you think is right and how shall we resolve this within the playgroup?

A You are right. One of the ways in which young children's minds differ from the minds of adults is that much of their inner equilibrium depends on getting what they want when they want it. This is a normal state of affairs and will be outgrown if handled correctly—that is, with understanding and sensitivity.

Unfortunately, many parents are told that if they do not force children to act with the social manners and graces of adults, their children will remain "self-centered." But when parents try to force children to act in ways that are more grown-up than they can handle, children feel inadequate. To comfort themselves, they cling even more tenaciously to getting what they want when they want it. So the irony is that expecting two-year-olds to share and not grab actually makes them more desperate to hang on to what they have and to go for another child's possessions.

On the other hand, if parents respond with gentleness and understanding to their young children's acquisitive behaviors, their children learn that they can't always have what they want, but that they can always count on their parents' love and admiration. This helps them to grow out of the need to get what they want when they want it. When two-year-olds are allowed to be two-year-olds, their normal maturation causes friendships to become more important to them than possessions by the time they are three or four years old. They want to share as a way of maintaining and enjoying friendships. In other words, grabbing and refusing to share are normal two-year-old behaviors that will be outgrown if they are responded to with kindness and are not censored.

We suggest the following guidelines for playgroups:

- All parents involved should recognize that it is normal for two-year-olds to refuse to share and to want to grab other children's toys.
- Children who won't share should not be made to feel badly or be forced to share.
- Children who grab will have to give the toy back if the other child is unhappy, but they should not be made to feel badly, and every attempt should be made to comfort them. For example, a parent might say, "I know how much you wanted that toy, but Alice is playing with it now. Let's give it back and I'll help you find something else fun to do."
- Whenever possible, try to provide multiples of the most desirable toys. Or, if a particular toy provided the occasion for much squabbling the last time, put it away before the other children arrive.

Why won't my baby give her older brother a break?

Q I have a 3-year-old and a 1-year-old. Most of my friends are having difficulty getting their older children to be nice to the younger ones. My problem is that my younger child is making life impossible for the older one. She follows him around, grabs any toy he is playing with, sits practically on top of him whenever he is playing with something, and generally never gives him a minute's peace. The older child is fundamentally very loving with his little sister, but he is becoming increasingly impatient and irritable. Suggestions?

A Yes—jump in to protect your son without imposing unfair expectations on your daughter. A 1-year-old cannot understand that her brother, whom she loves being with, needs time to himself. Trying to explain this will either hurt her feelings or make her redouble her efforts to be close to him. When your daughter heads for her brother, scoop her up, take her in another room and read or play with her. If you don't have time to play, stick her in her high chair and give her some pots to bang on

Explain to your son that his sister wants to be with him every moment because she loves him, but that you can understand he needs some space from her and that you will make that happen. Then be sure you spend some special time with your son, who, after all, is still young himself and needs time with you.

Big brother needs a lighter touch

Q I have a four-week-old and a three-year-old and I am a little concerned because the three-year-old can be rather rough in the guise of "loving" the baby. He hugs her too hard, holds her hand too tightly and bounces her up and down too roughly. I have told him over and over how delicate babies are and that a boy as strong as he is can really hurt her, but his behavior doesn't seem to change. If I tell him he can't hold the baby, he gets hysterical, but I worry about the baby's safety. Please tell me what to do.

A There are two conflicting issues here—your three-year-old's feelings about having a new sibling, and keeping the baby safe. The baby's safety takes precedence. No matter how upset your son gets when you tell him he can't hold her, if he hurts her, he may be more upset. This feeling will be deeper and more permanent. So closely supervise your son's interactions with his sister. Never leave them alone together and be especially careful to keep him with you while she is sleeping. If he holds her too tightly, simply take her away saying, "It seems as though you are finding it difficult to be gentle with your sister, so I will hold her." If he cries, tell him gently but firmly that for his sake and the baby's you can't allow him to hurt her. If he promises to be more careful, you decide whether he can control himself at that moment.

Help your son recognize and share his negative feelings about his sister as well as show him she hasn't robbed him of your love. Tell him all big brothers and big sisters sometimes feel angry at babies and it's important to talk to you about those feelings and not take them out on his sister. There are many excellent storybooks describing the mixed feelings siblings have, such as "A Baby Sister for Frances," by Russell Hoban. When your son feels safe enough to tell you he "hates" his sister, don't be outraged. Accept his feelings– "I know you feel that way sometimes, just like all big brothers."

Also, your son has to see that his sister hasn't appropriated all of your affection. Use the baby's nap times to give your son a good dose of undivided attention and he will be much less resentful of the new arrival.

Sibling preparation

Q Do you have any suggestions on how to prepare a three-year-old for a new sibling?

A First, keep in mind that in spite of all your efforts, your child will still be in for a shock when the baby comes. Even so, there is a lot you can do to get your child used to the idea of a new sibling

Take your daughter to visit your friends who have babies, and read her books that describe how children her age felt about the new arrival. The more real you can make the unborn baby the better, so show your three year old a "picture" of the baby if you have an ultrasound, and as your pregnancy progresses let her feel the baby kick. See if she would like to help you to set up the baby's room, but don't force her to contribute her own baby toys, as that is one sure way to get the sibling relationship off on the wrong foot!

As your daughter realizes that you are carrying a real baby, you can also expect a barrage of questions about how the baby was made, how it got in there, how it will get out, etc. Keep your answers short and simple and let your daughter ask follow-up questions if she wants to know more. Most important, tell your daughter frequently how much you love her and how lucky the baby will be to have such a wonderful big sister. Let her know that even though the baby will take a lot of time, that you will be sure to set aside "special time" just for the two of you.

When to ask kids to share a bedroom

Q We have two boys, ages five and two. They currently sleep in separate bedrooms, but we are considering having them share a room in maybe another year or so. We would like to know your opinion on the best age to make this transition, as we have visions of all-night giggle fests, etc., but know that it can be done. Thank you.

A You don't say why you want them to share a room. If you don't need the space and are thinking it would be nice to have the brothers sleep together, we suggest that you get bunk beds for each of their rooms. That way, if they are getting along and want to sleep in the same room, they have the option. On the other hand, if they are having a bad day and there is a lot of squabbling going on, or if they are keeping each other up so late that they are not getting enough sleep, they can stay in their separate rooms and have peace and a good night's sleep.

If you need to reclaim one of the boys' rooms for some reason, we suggest that you wait until your younger son is four or five. Two- and three-year-olds can find it very difficult to settle down for the night even when they are exhausted and are in their own room. If an older brother with a later bedtime is playing an exciting game or even just walking in and out of the room, they may have a very hard time getting to sleep. By four or five, children go to sleep more like adults, that is they are more capable of lying in bed doing a quiet activity until they fall off to sleep. They are also more aware of whether they are tired. However, even four- and five-year-olds can get overstimulated by the presence of activity going on around them at bedtime. So in general the longer you can defer the change, the easier it will be on you and on them.

Aggressive twin

Q I have three-year-old boy/girl twins. We have had a problem with aggressive behavior in my son directed towards his sister. He will rip toys out of her hands. He also hits her, especially when he is frustrated about something she is doing, or something she doesn't want to do that he does. She does not hit back, but says, "You cannot hit me!" I am not sure how to handle these aggressions using your guidelines. I've tried talking with him about it. I've tried removing him from the heat of the battle to a nearby chair, and I've tried removing him to his room. I don't feel at all comfortable with the isolation technique, but I am confused as to how to apply loving regulation to these heated, aggressive situations. I have tried just sitting next to him quietly while he "rages," hoping to show support. He usually pushes me away, though once in awhile he will come to me for hugs and cuddling after a few minutes of crying. At those times I feel like his own emotions and behavior scared himself, and he looks to me for comfort. I feel that at those times I'm able to communicate to him that I do love him even when he's upset. Will loving regulation eventually work but it takes time?

A Yes, do persevere in your compassionate approach because loving regulation will work for you and your son. Actually, there are really two separate issues here: how to use loving regulation when your son torments your daughter and how best to prevent this from happening. Obviously the best approach is prevention. In our experience, when one sibling is overly aggressive toward another it is often because that sibling feels that he is fighting for scarce resources – his parents' attention. This is particularly likely in the case of twins. If your son is regularly angry with your daughter, he may be feeling that his sister is getting attention that he needs and wants. We suggest that you begin by finding some time to spend alone with each twin each day. While this is a challenge with twins, who are on the same schedule, maybe you have friends, relatives, or a babysitter who can occupy one while you spend time with the other. We think you will be amazed at how much better your son will treat your daughter if he can count on time alone with you.

Another form of prevention is to note at what times of day or under what circumstances your son tends to pick fights. Then try to occupy him with an enjoyable project as those situations approach.

At those times when, in spite of all your efforts, your son becomes aggressive toward your daughter, do continue to use loving regulation. That is, protect your daughter by restraining your son while at the same time you offer him loving arms and caring words. There is a misguided notion that being kind to children who are "misbehaving" encourages the misbehavior. Nothing could be further from the truth. Your ongoing kindness provides a model of relating that your son will emulate. On the other hand, when parents respond punitively toward a misbehaving child, the child copies the harsh response and learns to treat himself and others punitively. So a punitive response actually strengthens a child's aggressive behavior, and a kind response makes it less likely to occur.

♥

Constant sibling bickering requires individual attention

Q I have two boys, ages three and two. I know you don't advise having children so close together, but the second son was not planned. All they seem to do is fight. They want the same toys and all my attention. The younger one usually gets the worst of it, although he retaliates by ruining a building project or taking his brother's favorite stuffed animal. I send them to their rooms, give them time-outs and more often than I would like, end up screaming at both of them. I am absolutely at my wit's end. What do you suggest?

A Usually when siblings are fighting this persistently, each believes he is not getting enough parental attention and affection. If there is another parent, divide up and spend time with each of the boys, letting them experience some undivided attention and caring. Of course, if you are a single parent, then there is only one of you and satisfying the needs of two young children at the same time can be very difficult. But you can take advantage of times when one of the boys is sleeping, at preschool or at a friend's house. Resist the temptation to use that time to get chores done and instead use it to give the other boy some alone time. Filling each of the boys with love and affection is the most effective way to get them to stop fighting.

In the meantime, though, there are some strategies that might minimize the mayhem. For now, buy toys in duplicate to cut down on the squabbling. When fighting starts, rather than screaming or giving time-outs, try keeping first one, then the other, boy by your side. Find them something to do or enlist them in your activity if possible (they can help vacuum, dust or do other chores).

Cooperative activities that require both boys to "pull together," such as cooking where one pours and one stirs, can also cut down on friction. If you stick with this approach and add your own creative tactics, you will increasingly find that the boys are getting along better and perhaps even becoming good friends.

Jealous toddler is simply acting her age

Q I have three girls, ages six, four and two. The problem is my two-year-old. At family birthdays, she melts down. She wants to open every present and play with them before the recipient has a chance. We have tried explaining to her it's not her birthday and that she will have presents when it is her birthday, but that doesn't seem to help. We end up sending her to her room, but meanwhile she has disrupted the fun of the birthday child. Our four-year-old is turning five in a few weeks and we wonder if you have any suggestions for how to handle the two-year-old.

A Actually, your two-year-old is behaving quite normally for her age. The challenge is to manage her behavior to keep her and everyone else happy. Two-year-olds lack the capacity either to vicariously enjoy a sibling's pleasure at getting presents or to sooth their desire to have presents now with the notion that they will have a birthday in the future.

There is no point in trying to teach your daughter not to make a fuss when someone else is getting presents because she is simply too immature to feel comforted by the idea that it will be her turn someday. The best approach is to make sure she has a few small presents to unwrap and open. For example, give her a set of blocks or plastic animals and wrap each individually so she has plenty of gifts and gift-unwrapping to keep her busy. That way she will be peacefully occupied when the birthday girl opens her presents and everyone will enjoy the occasion.

Will my three-year-old ever get along with the baby?

Q I have a six-week-old and a three-year-old and although I was looking forward to the new baby, my three-year-old is turning the experience into a nightmare. He pitches a fit whenever I have to do something with the baby, yells that I don't love him anymore, says his life is "horrible" since "he" came. I'm afraid to leave him alone with the baby for fear he might hurt him. Before the baby was born I had visions of the two of them becoming best friends. At this point I'll just be happy if my older boy ignores the baby. What do you suggest?

A Your older son is feeling displaced and he blames the new arrival who is taking up so much of your time. When you get angry at your son for trying to let you know how he feels, it makes him more certain that he has lost his place in your heart.

The answer is to do everything you can to make him feel included and to let him know that you love him as much as ever. Make special time for him every day while your husband watches the baby and have your husband do the same while you baby-sit. Enlist his help with the baby in ways that will make him feel he is your partner. For example, ask him to carry bags of baby supplies from the store and compliment him on his strength.

When the baby needs attention, try to engage your older son in singing songs or telling stories so he doesn't feel so left out. When he complains about the baby, agree that right now it's frustrating that he can't have as much of your attention as he once did. Most important, do your best not to lose your temper at him, but to be especially kind and tender.

How can we best prepare our firstborn for the arrival of the new baby?

Q We have a 10 1/2-month-old who will be 15 ½ months old when our new baby arrives. What can we do to prepare her (as best we can) for the new arrival? How do we help her accept the new baby.

A There's probably no way to totally prepare a 15-month-old for the arrival of a new baby, but there are things you can do to help her accept the arrival of her new sibling. It will help to take her to visit friends who have babies; to read her simple books about the arrival of siblings; to tell her that inside Mommy's round shape is a new baby brother or sister that she can't see, but she can feel; and to show her a "picture" of the baby if you have had an ultrasound.

Most important, though, is to realize that, most likely, your daughter will be amazed, briefly amused, and then somewhat put out by the new arrival. The best way to help her accept the new baby is to give her as much love and attention as you can spare and to be accepting of her negative feelings, including wishes that the new arrival would disappear as suddenly as she came Above all, please realize that your child is at a stage of needing a lot of focused attention from you. Your responsiveness is the yardstick by which she judges her own self-worth. For this reason, it will mean the world to your daughter if you can find ways to love and care for the new baby without making your daughter go too long without your loving attention. For example, you can sing songs with her during diaper changes, read to her while you nurse or bottle feed, and hold her and play with her while the new baby is napping. And, hopefully, you and your spouse have friends and family who can watch the baby occasionally to free you both to spend more time with your daughter.

While finding the energy to satisfy both a baby and a toddler may seem like a daunting task, the extra effort you make now will pay off later. Most importantly, you will protect your daughter from viewing the baby as a rival who is robbing her of her greatest joy—your attention. This is the best way to help her accept her new sibling.

What your kids can do to help with the baby

Q How do we encourage a positive relationship between our two older kids (18 months and 6 years) and the new baby? What are some baby-care skills the two older siblings can do?

A It sounds as though you have your hands full with two older children and a baby, and we can certainly understand your wish to have the older siblings lend a hand. Yet the best way to help siblings become best friends is to show them that the newcomer hasn't robbed them of the most precious thing in their world—your time and attention. While you undoubtedly feel burdened right now, if you can find the space to pay attention to your other two children while you are diapering, feeding or rocking the baby, they will be more likely to take a kindly attitude toward the new arrival.

The six-year-old will probably find it easier to understand your need to spend a lot of time with the baby and will also be more likely to find pleasure in helping you. Children that age can be of genuine assistance—they can push the stroller, help with baths, run to get a diaper, shake on baby powder, etc. In contrast, 18-month-olds are like newborns in that their sense of security and inner contentment is still entirely dependent on your positive attention. As a result, your 18-month-old lacks the emotional reserves to wait with equanimity while you attend to the new baby.

The best strategy is to include your toddler whenever possible—let him sit on your lap whenever it is free or sing with him when it is not. Also, your partner can make a lasting contribution by giving the older children time with him and by caring for the newborn while you snuggle or play with them. While it can feel a bit overwhelming to be indispensable in so many lives, the more you both can give now, the more you will be repaid later by the secure, happy, confident outlook that your love and attention will instill in your older children.

Waking up at night

Q In anticipation of a new baby in May, my husband and I moved our two-year-old from his crib to a bed about a month ago. He immediately fell in love with his "big boy bed" and we have had no problems at all with him trying to get out when we lay him down for the night. However, for the past week or so he's been getting up at various times of the night and coming into our room, thinking it's time to get up, when it's actually anywhere from 11:00 p.m. to 4:00 a.m.

We tell him that it's not time to get up yet and he willingly goes back to his own bed, but I like to go with him to make sure he gets his blankets on so he doesn't get too cold during the night. Is there any way to teach our two-year-old when it's time (or not time) to come in and wake us up?

Thanks. I love the advice in your column!

A Even if you could teach your two-year-old when it was time to get up—for example, you told him it wasn't time to get up until it is light out—that knowledge would not affect his desire to come and see you when he wakes. The good news is that your son is willing to go back to bed and back to sleep; not every two-year-old is so accommodating. We recommend that you do not make a big deal of his coming in. This is a phase he will outgrow as long as it doesn't result in a power struggle.

In addition, since this awakening is new, ask yourself if there are changes in his waking life that could be concerning him. Has there been a major shift in home or school routines? Is a loved person or pet ill? Has a friend moved away? If you do think of events that might be upsetting him, bring them up and ask if he is feeling sad or bothered.

Obviously the most likely explanation is that he is increasingly aware that there is a sibling residing inside of you who gets to be right next to you all night long. He may understandably be feeling rather left out. If you make it possible for him to talk with you about his feelings, they will be less likely to awaken him in the night.

♥

Should I force my son to give up his crib?

Q I have a 2½-year-old son and a newborn daughter. Before our daughter was born, we convinced our son to give up his crib and move to a youth bed. He chose a car bed and really seemed to like it.

Once his sister arrived and started sleeping in his crib, however, he wanted to sleep in the crib again, too. If we don't watch him, he climbs in with her and whenever she is out of the crib, he gets in and pretends to sleep. At night he cries and says he hates his bed.

We have tried to tell our son that he is a big boy in the family and that's why he gets the special bed, but he puts his hands over his ears and shrieks. This conflict is driving us crazy, especially since we are already short on sleep because of the baby. How can we convince him to accept the bed?

A Even though he was attracted by the idea of the car bed, it seems your son wasn't really ready to give up his crib, especially to a newcomer who is getting attention that used to belong entirely to him.

We suggest you leave his car bed in his room and borrow a crib for the time being. Give your son back his old crib and put your newborn in the borrowed crib. This will make your son happy and show him that his needs are not being shoved aside by the new baby.

Once he has the option of sleeping in his crib, you may find that he increasingly chooses to sleep in the bed. But since this was such a sensitive issue for him, let him choose the timing for removing the crib.

If you respond to him this way, he will be more relaxed, will resent the baby less and will be more likely to enjoy the role of big brother.

♥

Getting toddlers to stay in their beds at night

Q Am I spoiling my 2½-year-old daughter by letting her stay up late? Her older sibling's bedtime is 8:00 p.m. She used to go to bed so nicely when she was still in her crib, but now it's a struggle every evening and she usually wins the battle.

A It's really not a question of whether you are "spoiling" your daughter, but of making sure that your daughter gets enough sleep. Parents are often misadvised that granting children's wishes "spoils" them. Actually, when you grant your child's wishes whenever possible, she will find it much easier to understand and tolerate the times when her desires must go unmet and she will grow up to be generous toward others.

Applying this principle to your daughter's bedtime, if she goes to bed at 8:00 p.m., the same time as her older sibling, but sleeps eleven or twelve hours, or sleeps a little less but takes a good afternoon nap, she is getting enough rest. In that case, there is nothing to be gained and much to be lost by fighting with her to get to bed at 7:00 p.m. when she would go happily at 8:00 p.m.

However, if the family rhythm dictates that she get up early in the morning, and she needs to be in bed before 8:00 p.m. in order to get enough rest, do what you can to make the transition pleasant. Separate her from her sibling and spend some "special time" in her room with her half an hour before her bedtime. Let her choose what games she would like to play or what stories she would like you to read. Then create a fun ritual for when she is in bed. Music or story tapes are often effective at keeping two-year-olds in bed. If in spite of all your efforts she climbs out of bed and comes to your room, walk her back to bed in a friendly way.

We should add that the difficulty you are having is the reason we suggest keeping children in cribs until they are at least three years old. When two-year-olds are moved into regular beds, they often find it difficult to stay put.

Full-time mom with part-time job needs rest

Q My three kids, ages five, three and eight months, are often awake every morning before 6:30 a.m. Besides being a full-time mom, I also work a part-time night shift and I do not want to wake up at 6:30 a.m. every morning. (They used to sleep until almost 8:00 a.m.) Usually, it's the three-year-old who wakes up first, and then wakes everybody else up. When I tell him to go back to bed, he screams and cries and there is no reasoning with him, which makes me scream and cry, and that is a horrible way to start the day. If I tell him he may play quietly in his room until the rest of us are awake, he makes noise anyway, as any three-year-old would. I think I'm going crazy. I am exhausted and irritable all the time and feel like all I do lately is snap at my kids. My husband, who wakes up at 4:30 a.m. for work, has little sympathy for me or this situation. I am at my wit's end. What can I do to get my kids to sleep longer, short of keeping them awake until midnight?

A With three children under five and a part-time night job you definitely have your hands full. You are accurate in believing that something in your life needs to change—you are not getting adequate rest, and this lack of sleep is affecting you in destructive ways. However, your kids are not the problem-they are acting like kids. It is not unusual for children five, three and eight months to wake up about 6:30 a.m. The real solution is to find a way to get yourself more sleep. Perhaps you have a neighbor or relative who could watch your children for an hour or two so you can nap. Or maybe you could switch to a daytime shift. If all else fails, when the eight-month-old is taking a nap maybe you could settle the three- and five-year-old down to watch a video and get a little rest.

Most important is to do something—these are important, formative years for your children and, as you clearly realize, you need to feel up to caring for and enjoying them.

My toddler is a terror: Is something wrong with him?

Q How do you suggest we handle our 2½- year-old's aggressive behavior at the playground. Tim marches up to a child who has a toy he wants, grabs it and then refuses to give it back. I have to physically take it away from him and hand it back to the other child. Then he tries to grab it again. If another child wants one of his toys, he hangs on to it and screams. I try to talk to him about sharing but he won't listen. The other thing is he won't wait his turn – he actually has tried to push other children off the stairs to the slide so he can get on faster. Again, he pays no attention when we try to explain the importance of taking turns. At home with us, he's a very loving and sweet boy, but we are worried about this antisocial behavior and don't know how to deal with it.

A You are witnessing normal two-year-old behavior. Your son is at an age when he wants what he wants when he wants it regardless of who or what is standing in his way.

Trying to get him to share is counterproductive. He will react by becoming even more attached to his toys and more suspicious of other children; that is, he will become less, not more altruistic.

If he grabs another child's toy or tries to push children out of the way to get to the slide, the goal is to manage his behavior in a friendly manner, to use loving regulation. Gently return the toy and try to find him something else to play with or comfort him when he cries. Pick him up off the slide and tell him in an understanding tone that you know it's hard to wait, but he can't push other children.

Once you realize his "antisocial" behavior is age-appropriate, you can see that it makes no sense to become angry or disapproving. Your son will outgrow this phase and want to share and take turns because his friends will have become more important to him than any toy.

When can you reason with a two-year-old? Never

Q What do you do when you are putting a two-year-old to bed and you have promised to read two stories and she begs and begs for more? Before I start reading, I say, "Just two books, right?" and she smiles angelically and says, "Wite." But when I finish the second book, she starts demanding, "More, more, more." No matter how many times I remind her that she agreed she would go to bed after two stories, she shakes her head and insists I read more. If I don't give in she has a tantrum, but if I keep reading the process just goes on and on. It has gotten to the point that I am tempted to just leave her to have a fit by herself, but I know from your column you don't advise doing that, and I have always agreed with your logic. Suggestions?

A The problem is you are trying to reason with a two-year-old. Two-year-olds not only want what they want when they want it, but they assume they can get what they want when they want it. In other words, because they are normally both impulsive and cognitively immature, two-year-olds cannot be overpowered by logic, and it is really not fair to get angry or punish them for acting their age.

We suggest loving regulation, which means managing your daughter's behavior while you continue to offer affection and closeness. Tell her you will read her two stories without making her promise not to ask for more. She will never be able to keep the promise. After the first story, say in a friendly way, "OK, we're going to read the last story now." After the second story ends, offer some sort of nighttime ritual such as songs, hugs and kisses.

If she cries because she can't have another story, tell her you know it's difficult to go to bed when she wants more stories, but that she needs her sleep and you will read more first thing in the morning. If she continues to cry, hold her until she stops and then go back to putting her to bed. Your daughter will get enough sleep and she will have learned a valuable lesson, namely that even when she can't have what she wants, she can count on having a loving relationship with you.

Loss of an attachment object

Q My son (sixteen months old) lost his pacifier and we tried to give him the spare. He refuses and throws tantrums. He wants the pacifier but knows that it is not the same one. How can we get him to take a new pacifier?

A In general, when a young child is passionately attached to a pacifier or a stuffed animal, it is a good idea to introduce duplicates as soon as possible in order to avoid just the situation you are describing. But this strategy obviously will not help at this point.

The problem now is that, like all children his age, your son believes that you are all powerful and, therefore, that you could produce the pacifier if you wanted. So his tantrums are the result both of the loss of his favorite pacifier and also of his belief that you are refusing to find it and return it to him.

We suggest that you make a dramatic show of searching for the pacifier and then show your son that you feel disappointed because you cannot find it. Then try offering him the substitute once again. Eventually, he will probably accept it, but in the meantime comfort him as much as possible. Showing him with lots of hugs and soothing words that you want him to feel better will also help to counteract the hurt your son feels as a result of his immature (but normal) belief that you are keeping his pacifier from him.

How can I help my toddler feel OK about his surgery?

Q My 1½-year-old son has to have surgery to correct a hernia. He can only have liquids for the day before the surgery and will have restricted activity after the surgery. He is a very active little boy and I know this will be hard on him. Also I am worried that he will be traumatized by the procedure. What can my husband and I do to make the whole experience as benign as possible for him?

A The key is to make yourself available to your son during and immediately after the procedure. There are numerous ways to prepare your son for the surgery. Buy some of the excellent books for young children who have to go to the hospital and read them to him at bedtime for a week or two before his surgery.

Explain to him that, just as in the books, the doctors will be fixing something inside his skin. Tell him it won't be fun, but once it's over everything will be all right. Have the doctor explain exactly what will happen and then choose a doll or one of his favorite stuffed animals and recreate as much of the procedure as possible, including X-rays, intravenous tubes and anesthesia. Then, let him play doctor and "fix" the toy himself. Answer his questions as simply but accurately as possible.

Finally and most important, make sure that you or his father are with him during the time he is in the hospital. Most doctors will now allow parents to be with young children until they are anesthetized. This will make the procedure much less frightening for your son.

Stay with him for as long as he has to remain in the hospital and accept tears or complaining as legitimate responses to the unpleasantness he has had to undergo. When he comes home, make a welcome home party with balloons and a few presents to recognize that he went through something difficult and to celebrate that the operation is behind him.

How do I correct without doing harm?

Q My twenty-month-old daughter is beginning to try saying a lot of words. Sometimes she makes a mistake and calls something by the wrong word. More often, she badly mispronounces the word she is trying to say.

I want to correct her so she doesn't keep making the same error, but I have learned enough from reading your column to know that I don't want to do anything to shake her confidence in herself. What would be an appropriate response when she misuses or mangles words?

A Your daughter is so young that you don't have to be concerned about her mistakes—you can just enjoy the process of her language acquisition. All toddlers misuse and mangle words in the process of learning them. Your role is to be upbeat about whatever effort she makes and to simply model the correct pronunciation or usage. For example, if she says, "at" for "cat," you might reply, "Yes! That's right, that's the cat!" She will feel warmed by your enthusiasm at the same time she absorbs the correct pronunciation because she loves imitating you.

My two-year-old won't listen when I explain anything

Q I know two-year-olds can be very difficult to deal with, but I am really having trouble with my daughter. Whether it be wearing her seat belt, not bothering her older sister when doing homework or not eating the food she picks up from the sidewalk, she resists. When I explain why, she yells louder and gets more and more upset. On occasion, I have lost my temper and slapped her bottom, which makes her scream louder and makes me feel terrible, because I don't believe in hitting children. I don't seem to able to get her to do what she has to without a complete meltdown—on both our parts. What do you suggest?

A We suspect the real problem here is that you are trying to reason and be reasonable with a two-year-old, which is not really possible. Two-year-olds don't have the language skills necessary to understand hypothetical statements ("If you eat that piece of candy you found on the sidewalk, you could get sick") or to argue with explanations. Moreover, they have very little impulse control—they want what they want when they want it. This is a normal state that they will outgrow, but for now words will not solve the problem.

Because your two-year-old is behaving normally, there is no reason to punish her or to be angry with her. The real solution is to realize explanations are not going to work and solve the problem in a friendly but expeditious manner (take the candy and throw it away, strap her into her car seat, pick her up and take her away from her sister). Then you can comfort her and try to help her engage in an enjoyable activity. You will not have the same frustrations. And you will be much less likely to lose your temper. Also, keep in mind the goal of anticipating and preventing your two-year-old's meltdowns (have a toy to give her when you put her in her car seat, have your older daughter keep her door closed when she is doing homework, keep an eye out for attractive garbage and change course).

Help your child choose to lose the diaper

Q My daughter is three-years-old and is still in diapers. She has used the potty once or twice but she immediately asked for her diapers and has shown no interest since. It is a problem because I hate to send her to play with other children and make their parents change her diapers. Also, she is enrolled in a preschool for the fall that will only take children who are trained. My husband and I have offered her all kinds of rewards for using the toilet, and she shows interest in getting the rewards but then doesn't come through. I have asked her why she doesn't want to use the potty and all she says is, "I don't know." We are pretty much at our wit's end over this. What do you advise?

A The reason we use the term "toilet choosing" instead of "toilet training" is that the child really does have to choose to use the toilet. Trying to pressure children into giving up diapers usually leads to power struggles, rebellion, and, as a result, even more delay. The good news is that all healthy children will eventually choose the potty over diapers.

Even though it is inconvenient that your daughter remains in diapers, pressuring her will only delay the moment when she will choose to use the potty. We suggest that you also avoid rewards, which are actually a subtle kind of pressure and rarely work well. There are a few positive strategies for encouraging your daughter to make the transition. Regularly invite children over for play dates. Children at this age are great imitators of other children and if her friends are all using the potty, she may too. Substitute pull-ups for diapers, so that she can experiment with the potty on her own. Buy her some pretty underwear and let her wear it if she wants. She may decide on her own that she would like to keep it dry and clean.

Even though it may seem at times like the proverbial elephant in the room, try not to focus on this issue. Children mature on different timetables. It is important for your daughter's emotional development that you give her the space to make her own choice to use the potty. Then when she does make the transition, she will also experience an increased self-confidence that will carry over into other areas of her life.

How do I convince my son he isn't ready for big boy pants?

Q My 2½-year-old is holding his bowel movements. We took him to the pediatrician and there is nothing physically wrong. He asked to wear "big boy" pants like his older brother and said he wanted to go in the potty, but has not been able to. He waits until his diaper is on at night and usually has a bowel movement then. But during the day, he says his stomach hurts. When we suggest he would feel better if he went in the potty, he shakes his head no. How can we get him to feel more comfortable with the potty?

A Your son seems to have asked for the "big boy" pants before he was ready. He wanted the pants, but didn't realize it meant actually using the potty. Now he is in a conflict he can't resolve.

The only constructive way out is to tell your son you understand how much he wanted to wear big boy pants, but that you don't think he's quite ready so you are going to put him back in diapers or pull-ups for a while. He may protest, but we are quite sure he will be relieved.

Will our 3-year-old ever use the potty?

Q We have a 3-year-old who is not yet toilet trained. We took the laid-back approach, but enough is enough. We are really tired of diapers and we also have a new baby coming in a few weeks and the thought of two children in diapers is discouraging. But nothing seems to be working. We have tried reading him books about children using the potty, offering him treats as rewards and taking our son to the house of other little boys who are trained. He couldn't be less interested. Our pediatrician says there is nothing wrong with him. I have noticed, though, that he seems to be having fewer bowel movements, so I have been giving him a children's laxative. Please help.

A The problem is that children cannot be cajoled or pressured into using the potty—it is a purely voluntary action. Without meaning to, you have gotten into a power struggle you can't win, your son is reacting by rejecting the potty and now by holding his bowel movements. Your son is going to have to want to use the potty, which is why we like to use the term "toilet choosing" rather than "toilet training." The sooner you take all the pressure off and let him feel it is truly his choice, the sooner he is likely to want to be like his friends and leave diapers behind. Also, when children who are physically normal hold their bowel movements, it often means that they are reacting to pressure to use the potty by concluding that the problem could be avoided altogether if only they could keep from having bowel movements at all. This "solution" can become chronic and lead to further emotional and physical problems. The answer is not to force bowel movements through laxatives, but to remove the reason for the bowel-retention by letting your son know that you are content to let him choose to use the potty on his timetable rather than yours. While we can understand your frustration at the thought of having two children in diapers, it is also true that children about to have siblings cling to babyish ways—so your son is unlikely to graduate to the potty until after the baby is born.

Toilet choosing

Q My three-year-old son is not using the toilet yet, except on isolated occasions. I'm not concerned about it for the most part and don't want to pressure him into it. However, there is so much advice about toilet training that I'd like to hear whether you think that this is something that a child will pursue completely on his own, or to what extent can parents help the process along without making the child feel like he is being pressured into something for which he's not ready. For example, sometimes my son really doesn't want me to change his poopy diaper. It takes him away from playing and he seems to see it as a big distraction in general. Sometimes I say that someday when he's ready, he'll poop in the potty and then we won't have to change diapers at all, but for now we need to keep changing diapers so he doesn't get a rash. Is this saying too much?

A Your instinct that it is best to let your son make the choice to use the toilet is right on. This is why we use the term "toilet choosing" rather than "toilet training." Since no one can force another person to use the toilet, pressuring children to use the potty is counterproductive. Toilet wars alienate children from parents and, in the worst case, can lead to a serious medical problem termed encopresis, in which children try to avoid defecating at all. Because you are letting your child make the choice, when he does use the potty, he will feel proud and self-confident and close to you.

You didn't mention rewards, but so many parents wonder about them that we would like to mention that these are not a good idea. Rewards are a sign to children of how important using the toilet is to their parents. Also, rewards pressure children and make them feel bad and inadequate if they don't comply. Further, if children use the toilet to get the reward and to please parents, when they subsequently feel angry with their parents or the rewards cease, the toilet may become a means to express anger or to negotiate for goodies. If choosing the toilet becomes something your child does for you or for a reward, your child will miss out on the real goal of toilet choosing, which is the sense of pride and enhanced competence he will get from choosing to regulate important bodily functions.

You obviously are very sensitive to your son's need to make this choice for himself. It is fine to mention to him when he complains about having his diaper changed that he might want to try to use the potty. Just continue to avoid pressuring him into making the inevitable choice to use the toilet. You can be sure that even though you allow your son to choose to use the toilet on his own time table, he will not go to high school or be married wearing diapers!

♥

Refusal to go anywhere

Q My 3-year-old is starting to take her clothes off when she doesn't want to go somewhere. What do you suggest?

A You have a very creative child; she has already figured out that you won't take her out of the house undressed! First, make a mental distinction between trips that your daughter must make (a visit to the pediatrician, accompanying you to pick up her brother) and trips that are elective (going to the park to play, a play date with a friend).

If a trip is mandatory, it is very important to communicate both that you understand your daughter's wish to stay home and also that there is no choice ("I can see you want to stay here, but we must go.") Give some thought to making the outing more palatable. ("We have to go to the doctor, but we can stop at the park on the way home.")

It is always preferable to avoid protracted conflict about the inevitable, so if all else fails, just pick her up in as friendly a manner as possible and start off. Try to make your intervention before the clothes come off, or at least as soon as you see your child going for the first shoe or sock. That way you will avoid the misery of trying to dress a kicking and screaming child.

If your daughter sheds her clothes to avoid an elective outing, we suggest that you simply say, "I think this is your way of letting me know that you don't feel like going. If you want to stay home, we can. Next time you want to stay home, all you need to do is to tell me." You can mention the fun your child will have on the trip out, but if she still resists, accept the decision with good grace and find something enjoyable for her to do at home. Next time you are planning an expedition, it might help to ask her ahead of time where she would like to go. In any event, she will be more willing to explore the world if you don't become negative with her at those times when she wants to stay home.

♥

We cannot get our toddler to cooperate at meals

Q Mealtimes are a nightmare at our house because our 2-year-old won't sit in his high chair. He squirms, arches his back and screams and, if we force him into the chair, he gets so hysterical he won't eat. If we give in, and put him in a regular chair at our table, he spills, pours and mixes his food all over the table and no one else can eat in peace. If we leave him out of the high chair, he runs off and he's not old enough to be in other parts of the house by himself. We are at our wits' end. Suggestions?

A It's all too true that 2-year-olds march to their own drummers and aren't always on the same schedule or program as the rest of the family. There are some things you can do to make sitting in a high chair more appealing to your son. Make sure not to feed him so many snacks that he loses his appetite by dinner; if possible don't have family dinner so near to his bedtime that he is exhausted; have some special high chair toys that he plays with only at mealtimes; and give him foods that require activity, such as mixing or dipping. Also, your son might prefer a toddler chair that attaches to the table or fits safely in larger chairs that will allow him to feel more a part of things, yet still keep him geographically contained. However, if these strategies and others you come up with yourself don't work, the reality is that fighting with your son and forcing him into his high chair will only make everyone miserable and, possibly, create chronic eating problems. It would be better to recognize that this problem is time-limited and delegate a different family member each night to watch him while others eat. Alternatively, as 2-year-olds often have fairly early bedtimes; wait, if possible, until he is asleep to have the family meal.

How do I get my toddler to behave in a nice restaurant?

Q I have three children, ages 8, 6 and 2 ½. My husband and I have always had a tradition of eating out on Sunday nights, and we like to eat at the kind of restaurant that has tablecloths and decent food. My 6- and 8-year-olds enjoy this, too, and are very well behaved. The problem is that our 2½ -year-old ruins the time for everyone. She throws food, silverware and anything else she can get her hands on. We bring toys for her, but she gets bored quickly and once she has eaten her fill (which takes about four minutes), she wants to get up. If we remove everything within her reach, she has a fit and starts screaming. We really don't want to have our Sunday dinner at a fast food restaurant, but this is not working either. Suggestions?

A At this moment you probably have only two good choices—get a babysitter or down-scale your restaurant choice. It would be a rare 2-year-old who could sit through the time it takes to eat at a nice restaurant, even with creative management. That said, there are some things you can do to lengthen the time your youngest is able to stay calm and content. For example, feed her food that takes a long time to eat (such as kernels of corn or tiny bits of meat), bring toys she hasn't seen before that fit on a high chair tray (paper and markers, cars or finger puppets), and enlist her older siblings to read to her or play with her. If all else fails, the adults can take turns taking her out of the dining room, where she can stretch her legs in the hall or lobby.

Will your philosophy hurt my child later?

Q My wife and I worry that if we follow your philosophy of child-rearing, our children will grow up entirely unprepared for the "real world." For example, if we give our toddler a hug instead of a time-out when he is throwing a tantrum, aren't we teaching him that he can get attention by having a fit? Doesn't it mean that when he gets older he'll expect other people not to care if he throws tantrums when he doesn't get his way? We get that it is more enjoyable to parent the way you suggest, but we're not clear that it prepares our children for the world.

A   There is no logical reason to try to prepare your toddler for the "real world." Just as it would be unthinkable to teach him calculus, this is not the moment in his development to try to get him to respond to frustration in an adult manner.

Your son has a child's mind and views the world very differently. For example, he believes the way you make him feel is the way he should feel. So if you isolate him when he has a tantrum, he believes that when he is upset he deserves to be alone and made to feel extra unhappy. As he grows older, he will be more likely to be unsympathetic toward himself and others in the face of life's inevitable frustrations. On the other hand, a comforting response to his tantrums will teach him to respond to frustration without losing his equilibrium.

Interestingly, there are numerous animal studies that support the claim that consistently warm responses to children actually prepare them better for the "real world." One recent study found that baby rats that were licked more by their mothers handled stress much better as adults. The increased maternal care activated a gene that regulated stress hormones and kept these hormones under control. So when your children are unhappy, comfort them knowing that you will be making them happier now and also helping them grow into stronger, more resilient adults.

What happens when the *Smart Love* method doesn't work?

Q   What do you suggest when the *Smart Love* approach doesn't seem to work? My husband and I have used your approach very successfully with our 1½-year-old toddler. However, we have a three-year-old who seems determined to provoke us. He continually asks for things he knows he can't have—soda, candy before dinner, to go outside when his sister is taking her nap—and then melts down when we say "no." We try the *Smart Love* approach of recognizing that it's hard when he wants something and can't have it and try to remain friendly and find him something else to eat or do that he will enjoy. That works for a while, but then he goes right back to demanding the impossible and throwing a fit when he can't have it. Eventually we lose our tempers and send him to his room for a timeout, but that doesn't seem to help, either. He throws things around his room or comes out looking for another confrontation. Please advise.

A Once children have unknowingly developed needs for conflict, these needs tend to be persistent. Without realizing it, your son feels comfortable and cared for when you become angry with him. When you use the *Smart Love* approach and help him with his frustration in a loving manner, initially he feels relieved and happy. Inevitably, through, he will be driven to provoke you again in an attempt to satisfy his needs to make you angry so he will feel loved and cared for. But when you become frustrated, lose your temper and send your son to his room, you are strengthening and perpetuating your son's confusion of anger and love.

On the other hand, if you respond to his provocations with consistent caring, eventually he will realize that closeness with you is preferable to conflict, and he will grow increasingly less provocative. We have found the *Smart Love* approach to be the most effective way to respond to children who have developed unrecognized needs for unhappiness, but you need to be patient. Your son developed these needs over the last three years, and it will be a while before he can turn away from them once and for all.

Chapter Three
Preschoolers and Kindergartners

♥

How to respond to strangers who ask insensitive questions

Q My four-year-old daughter, who was adopted when she was three-weeks-old, has a different racial heritage from my husband and myself. Our daughter is comfortable discussing her "different skin color" with us, but she gets very upset when we are out in public and people stop us and ask insensitive questions, such as: "Where did she come from?," "Who were her real parents?," or "How old was she when you got her?" She wants to know why people "don't think I belong with you."

I know people mean well and I don't want to be rude, but I don't want to upset my daughter further by answering. What can I say?

A It never fails to amaze us how often strangers ask parents very personal questions about their children in their children's presence, as though the children were either deaf or unfeeling. This is true not only when children have a different racial make-up from their parents, but also when they are visibly different from other children in any way (including having a disability or being very tall or short, fat or thin).

Your most important job is to show your child that you know she is upset by these questions and that you love her and will protect her. For example, you might say to the stranger, "That question is way too personal to discuss with someone we don't know. What I will say is that she is a wonderful child and we adore her."

When you are alone with your child, take the opportunity to emphasize that anyone who looked carefully would be able to tell that you are her mom and she is your daughter and that, in any event, the two of you know for certain that you belong together now and forever.

♥

"Who's your real mom?"

Q I am a single woman who adopted my daughter when she was 5½ months old. She is now a friendly, bright kindergartner who is doing well in school and at music lessons. I have been totally open with her about the fact that she is adopted.

How should she handle it when kids say, "That's not your real mom," and ask her what her real mom's religion was? We are Jewish. My child is Hispanic and was formally converted to Judaism shortly after I adopted her. When she says that I didn't give birth to her but I am her real mother, the kids keep badgering her about why she was given away.

When she says she doesn't want to discuss the topic, the kids sometimes accept that and sometimes don't. One kid told her that the reason she didn't want to talk about it was because she didn't know the answers and she should ask her mother. My kid is tired of the questions (and so am I, actually) and she seems mad with me that she is adopted. What's going on and what should we do?

A As a first step, we suggest that you make an appointment with your daughter's kindergarten teacher and alert her to the fact that your child is regularly upset because of her classmates' ignorance about the realities of adoption. Ask if she would lead some class discussions on the many ways in which families can be formed. When the teacher discusses adoption, she could mention some famous people who were adopted, and also emphasize that adopted children are not "given away" but are "given to" parents who are just the right people to raise them.

If the teasing persists, help your daughter to understand that she is being teased not because there is anything negative about having been adopted, but rather because the children teasing her can see that this topic upsets her. Remind her that other children would be bothered by being teased about different characteristics, such as their height. Explain that the best way to avoid being teased is not to show the teasers that she is bothered by their barbs, because children who tease get their enjoyment from getting a rise out of their victims.

Finally, if you haven't already done so, give your daughter a big hug and tell her how proud you are of the way she defended herself and her relationship with you.

Can I use *Smart Love* to help my special needs child?

Q Do *Smart Love* techniques work with kids with special needs, such as autism?

A Actually, we have found that the *Smart Love* approach is effective and growth-promoting for children of any age, including those with special needs and problems. Because the way children are treated becomes the model for how they treat themselves and others, all children benefit from a steady caring that meets their developmental needs. They also benefit when their behavior is managed in a friendly but firm way without attaching unpleasantness in the form of disciplinary measures such as timeouts or consequences.

It is often said that children with autism are "relationship blind," but in our clinical work, we have seen children who suffer from autism respond to positive, sensitive, non-intrusive care that builds on the child's particular interests or expressed motives.

Many autistic children can be helped to realize that relationships can be a source of comfort and joy. Once that developmental milestone is reached, these children often begin to make significant headway.

Professional help may be required to jump-start an autistic child's inborn wish for relationship pleasure and to help parents learn the most effective ways to relate to their child.

End battles over chores by making them fun for kids

Q We seem to be locked in an endless battle with our five-year-old son about doing chores. We make a list of chores for him to do each day and check off the chores he has done. If he does them all by the end of the week, he gets a gold star and we take him to his favorite restaurant. But he waits until the last minute to do his job and even then we have to nag him for what seems like an eternity. Instead of just doing the job, he says he is too tired, or lies and says he did it. I told him that he couldn't watch TV until he put the dirty dishes in the dishwasher and he slammed the dishes around until he broke one. I took away TV for a week and he cried and cried. The next day the fight started all over. I hate to see my son so angry and upset, but I also think he needs to take some responsibility around the house.

A Your goal is not that your son do any particular chore now, but that he take responsibility for his share of work when he is an adult. At that point, he will be on his own and gold stars will not have any effect. So the real issue is how to get him to enjoy doing his part today so he will continue to want to be helpful when no one is forcing him.

Both rewards and punishments are counterproductive because they are coercive. When you give rewards for chores, the message you send is the chore is unpleasant and the child has to be bribed to do it. When you punish the child for not doing the chore, you end up in a power struggle. When you force the child to do the chore, he resents it.

The best way to raise children to become adults who work willingly is to make chores enjoyable. To a five-year-old, that means doing chores while spending time with you. Most children who hate being told to pick up their toys will be happy to help you pick up the toys, especially if you make it fun (challenge him to see who can pick up the most toys or ask him which animal Mr. Elephant wants to sit next to as you put the toy on the shelf). Children fundamentally enjoy being with you and doing what you are doing—even if you're setting the table. Other chores are intrinsically fun, like washing the car or feeding the goldfish.

If a child doesn't feel like helping on a particular day, nothing of significance is lost as long as parents don't turn this temporary reluctance into a power struggle. Also, if your child really hates a particular chore, don't insist on it. Instead, try to find another job he will enjoy doing. Most important, keep in mind that your goal is to show your child that helping you with chores can be satisfying, not to force him to do work that he will never want to do when he is living on his own and can choose not to do it.

♥

How can we get our son to stay in bed?

Q My husband and I are at our wits' ends. We both work and hardly see each other during the day. Our 5-year-old son used to go to bed about 8:00 p.m., and then my husband and I could spend some time together. Recently, though, our son keeps coming out of his room and saying he needs a drink, his bear fell on the floor, he wants another story, etc. By the time we respond to all of his demands it is 10:00 p.m., and my husband and I are exhausted. We feel utterly irritated and frustrated. If we just tell him, "No, go back to your room," he refuses and sits on the stairs. A friend of ours suggests locking him in his room. We read your column regularly and have a feeling you won't agree to this, but what do you suggest?

A We understand your frustration, but you're right, it's not a good idea to lock children in their rooms. It is too frightening, it's potentially dangerous, and it sets a bad example for how to respond to disagreements. In reality, your son is not acting all that abnormally for his age—he hasn't seen you all day and he wants more of your company. Nonetheless, your son needs to get enough sleep and you and your husband do need time together.

We recommend that after work, you spend as much family time as possible in activities of your son's choosing. Your might consider pushing his bedtime back to 8:30 p.m. Then give him books or tapes that he can use in bed. Check to see if he needs a drink or a snack before he brushes his teeth. If he comes downstairs after his bedtime, walk him back to bed saying, "It's time for sleeping." If you are consistent, eventually he will realize there's not much to be gained in coming out of his room. Soon you and your husband should have your evenings back.

Our sons have grown apart, should I force them to play?

Q My best friend and I have sons the same age—they are both four years old. When the boys were infants and toddlers, my friend and I did everything with them. The problem now is that my son, Casey, no longer wants to play with her son, Sam. Sam is going through a fragile stage. If he can't have the toy he wants, he cries and throws toys and even tries to hit my son. My son says Sam is "no fun." I have tried telling him that it is just a phase and that Sam needs his help and understanding, but Casey remains convinced that he doesn't want to play with Sam anymore. If I bribe him with ice cream, he will allow me to invite Sam over, but then Casey is unhappy. I don't think Casey should be allowed to hurt a friend's feelings just because he is going through a difficult phase and I want to be able to continue to spend time with my friend. What do you advise?

A Your son is way too young to be expected to overlook his friend's consistently bad moods for the sake of your friendships. If Sam had only one or two bad days, certainly you could explain to Casey that everyone has a hard time now and then, so give Sam another chance. Given that Sam has been difficult to be with for some time, though, you need to acknowledge to your son that you can understand why he might not want to play with Sam right now. Your son is making an age-appropriate and healthy choice to want to play with children who don't cause a lot of conflict and unhappiness.

We suggest that you simply tell your friend that Casey and Sam seem to be in a period in which they will do better playing with others. Then make plans to see your friend alone at times when the boys' fathers can baby sit or the boys are in preschool or day camp.

Time for professional help?

Q Our son is six, and I have caught him twice now lighting fires in the corner of his room. He knows what he is doing is wrong. After the first incident, we punished him by taking away his video game for a week. Now, he has lit another fire. We will punish him again, but do you think this situation calls for a professional? His school counselor is recommending that we send him for some kind of emotional help but we are not certain whether this is necessary.

A The school counselor is giving you good advice. It is true that in most instances when children struggle with emotional problems or stresses, parents can help by changing their own behaviors and creating a closer relationship with their children. However, there are some behaviors that require immediate professional help. Fire-setting is one. Others are children who aren't speaking words by 2½, children who say they wish they were dead, children who deliberately hurt or kill animals or who repeatedly hurt other children, and children who regularly become hysterical and refuse to go when it is time for school. Children with these symptoms are experiencing a level of emotional discomfort that they can soothe only with self-destructive or aggressive behaviors. A caring professional can help them learn emotional pain can be soothed within a therapeutic relationship. At that point, their symptomatic behaviors will no longer be necessary.

We emphasize that your son is not setting fires as a way of manipulating you or bidding for attention. Children who have a free choice would not engage in dangerous activities to make their parents upset and angry. Your child needs understanding and professional help.

How can I handle a 5-year-old who bites?

Q I am concerned about my granddaughter. She is 5 years old and sometimes when she is frustrated and can't have what she wants, she bites the person who is thwarting her. My daughter responds by yelling at her and threatening to bite her back. Sometimes, she actually does sort of bite her. This has me very upset with both of them. I believe my granddaughter also is biting other children occasionally. Can you tell me what causes children to bite and how her parents should respond?

A Children bite as a way of expressing anger and frustration when they feel that talking about the problem is ineffectual. They need help to see that their concerns can and will be heard. When a parent bites back, it just teaches the child that biting is an acceptable response.

The most important strategy for dealing with biting is prevention. Watch the child and keep her teeth at a distance when she is upset or frustrated.

If she does try to bite, your daughter should hold the child so the child cannot reach her and say, "If you are angry, you can talk about it, but you cannot bite me." In this way, your daughter will prevent the biting and model a better way to handle frustration. It is crucial, though, that she listen in an understanding way when your granddaughter does verbally express angry or frustrated feelings in order to help the child develop outlets other than physical aggression.

Biting other children is a more serious problem because other children are unlikely to anticipate the biting or be able to deal with it the way an adult can—they can't hold the biting child at bay and may actually be bitten. Hopefully, if your daughter begins to respond differently, your granddaughter will stop biting other children. If she doesn't, professional help may be required.

Taking an all-or-nothing attitude

Q Your advice has been outstanding. I look forward to reading your columns every month in Chicago Parent magazine. I hope you can help me.

Our five-year-old son is a happy, wonderful child. There's one thing that concerns me. When he is upset (it does not matter if it is because we reprimanded him or told him we prefer not to invite certain children to our house) he adopts an all-or-nothing attitude. He will say things like "I'll never be able to do that." or "Nobody can come to our house. I'll never have any friends." We try to discuss this by telling him that we see that he is feeling frustrated or sad, but he just keeps it up. We end up getting frustrated and have to walk away, which only upsets him more. Once calmed down, he is fine.

What would you suggest as a better way to handle these moments? I would greatly appreciate any advice you have to offer. This has really upset me as I try to do the right thing.

A We think the problem is that, although you obviously love your son very much, you are too hard on him. What seems like a mere "reprimand" to you can feel devastating to a five-year-old.

Reprimands are a form of discipline and as such are counterproductive. Reprimanding your son makes him feel badly about himself and gives him the model of responding to disagreements with angry words. When he says, "I'll never be able to do that," he is mirroring what he perceives to be your negative feelings about him.

Rather than reprimands or other disciplinary measures, we suggest you adopt loving regulation as your way of managing your son's behavior. When you use loving regulation, you can remain kind and loving while you show your son what you want him to do. He will be convinced that you feel positively about him even when you need to alter his behavior. As a result, over time he will cease to feel that "I'll never be able to do that."

We don't know why you are preventing certain children from coming to your house, but your son appears to be terribly upset by this loss. We suggest you rethink your decision and only prohibit children who are physically or emotionally abusive. Your son clearly is at a vulnerable point in his development, and it is important that he experience you as being "on his side" and helping to further his friendships.

Finally, if your son is frustrated and sad, you don't need to talk him out of it. Most important is to stay with him and show him that you will be there for him until he feels better. Offer a hug, and if that is rejected, just sit with him until he calms down. Without meaning to, by walking away you give him the message that you don't like him when he is upset. The danger is that he will come to dislike himself for being upset. On the other hand, if you stick with him until he feels better, he will copy you and learn to be compassionate toward himself and others.

Should a six-year-old choose her wardrobe?

Q At what age do you recommend letting children pick out their own clothes? My six-year-old always wants to choose her clothes and most of the time they clash dreadfully, aren't appropriate (i.e., shorts in winter) or I can't stand to take her places in them. I have tried to educate her about what goes with what, but she seems to be deciding on whims like, "I wore these shorts on my birthday," or because they look to her like something she saw on TV. Sometimes she wants to wear fancy clothes to school and I think she will wreck them. Other times she wants to wear casual clothes to parties. We are fighting every day about her getting dressed. I have tried setting timers, and taking away treats when she doesn't get dressed, but when she gives in and gets dressed she is terribly mad and upset. I hate to keep starting the day like this, but I don't know what to do. Please help.

A The goal is to try to preserve your daughter's growing and age-appropriate wish to have more control over her life while at the same time keeping the necessary degree of oversight. We suggest that you have different drawers, bins, or areas of her closet for different purposes: school, parties and at home. Remove summer clothes in winter months, and vice versa, and store them somewhere else. Then invite your daughter to pick any clothes she would like from the appropriate bin. She will have the pleasure of choosing the look she wants, and you won't have to worry about her freezing or wearing clothes that are unsuited for the occasion. Please don't worry about clashing colors or odd combinations—it is good for your daughter to be able to exercise her creativity within the limits you have set.

How can I get my son to wear a costume?

Q My 3-year-old is really looking forward to Halloween, but he says he won't wear a costume. He insists that he doesn't want to "turn into someone else." I have suggested costumes of his favorite TV characters, such as Elmo, but he absolutely refuses.

His school has a Halloween parade, and trick-or-treating is very big in our neighborhood. I am afraid he will be teased for not having a costume and that some people will refuse to give him treats. This sounds like a small thing, but Halloween is really important to him. I worry that it will be a disaster. Any suggestions on getting him into a costume?

A This is not an uncommon fear among the 3-and-under set. Many children that age are afraid of what wearing a costume might do to them. There is no point in trying to reason or argue, because your son will outgrow his fear—probably by next Halloween. Rather, slip under his radar. Suggest that he go as himself, put a costume on the dog if you have one, or dress up yourself.

If any part of the family is in costume, there should be no problem with trick-or-treating. For the school parade, perhaps you can outfit a broom with a ghost costume so that he can bring the "costume" separately. If you let your creative juices flow, we are sure Halloween will be fun rather than frightening.

Patching up spats

Q Sometimes I worry I get too involved in trying to patch up my six-year-old daughter's spats with her friends, but I find it hard to stay detached when my child or her friend is in tears over an unintended slight or cross words. How do I achieve the right balance?

A Since you use the word "spats" to describe the quarreling, we assume that neither child is being hurt physically. If that were the case, intervention would definitely be called for. However, when the problem is hurt feelings, it is preferable to help your child learn constructive ways to handle the ups and downs of friendship than to try to patch up the disagreement yourself.

For example, if your daughter is upset because her friend has snapped at her, do acknowledge that it is painful when someone we care about is cross with us. At the same time, encourage her not to take her friend's irritability so personally. Suggest that she think about whether the friend had a bad day, or has been in a bad mood generally.

If your daughter has made her friend cry, ask if she thinks she might be taking out a bad mood or a bad day on her friend. It will be invaluable for her to learn that when she is grumpy she may feel irritable with everyone in her path, whether or not they deserve this response.

One way to help your child have smoother-running friendships is to keep play dates to a sensible length. If you notice that the children play well together for about two hours and then begin to fight, limit the visits to that amount of time.

Do realize that the inner well-being of all six-year-olds still depends to a large extent on having things go as they wish. Since your daughter's desires and those of her friends will sometimes clash, occasional tears and discontent are inevitable at this age.

Is my child too friendly?

Q I am concerned because when my son goes to a park, he tries to greet everyone at the playground. He turns four at the end of this month. Also, when some kids don't want to play with him, he starts talking to kids' parents. Some mothers are patient, but some mothers think he is a pest. What can I do to make him slow down, to have him play by himself and stop bothering other parents? I basically want him to be normal, independent and avoid possible rejection in the future. We came to the USA a year and half ago; we lived in Japan, where my son was born and grew up until the age of two. His mother is Japanese and I am Hispanic. The three of us are foreigners in this country. Thank you and I look forward to your response.

A Your son sounds like a wonderful, friendly child. It is a sign of how loved he feels by you that he trusts adults and enjoys conversing with them. Also, it is healthy that in response to temporary rejection from his peers he turns to other relationships for comfort rather than isolating himself. If there are parents at the park who can't appreciate and enjoy having a child strike up a conversation with them, that is their problem, not your son's. So stop worrying, enjoy your child, and feel happy that you are raising such an outgoing, trusting little boy.

Can empathy be taught?

Q Can empathy be taught? Are there different methods for children at different ages?

A That's a good question! Empathy is the ability to put yourself in another's place and to take that perspective into account in your relationship with the other person. Empathy is caring about the answer to the question, "How would I feel if I were in her shoes?" Unlike skills that require abstract thought, such as mathematics or reading, empathy is a way of relating to others. It cannot be taught formally, but is learned by imitating those who are important to us. Because your baby loves you, believes you are perfect, and wants to be just like you, she will grow up wanting to treat herself and others with the same loving kindness she gets from you. By understanding your child's needs and responding to them in a loving way, you teach her to understand and love herself and to understand and cherish others. Most important is to approach your child's development of the capacity for empathy in a relaxed way that accounts for her developmental immaturity.

Infants and young children normally base their well-being on their ability to get what they want when they want it. The toddler and preschooler who wants a toy will grab it, whether or not it is attached to another child, and she won't want to share a favorite toy with a friend who asks for it. This is normal behavior for her age, and you do not need to worry that if you don't come down hard on her she will grow up to be selfish and uncaring.

In reality, your child will not be ready to be a sharing, caring friend until after she turns three. At that point she will share because (most of the time) her friends will be more important to her than her possessions. So you needn't try to teach your child about the feelings and rights of others. Just continue to love, care for, and enjoy her. By imitating you, she will learn to treat others with the same consideration.

♥

Gentleness is the answer to kids' demands.

Q My husband and I are at our wits' end with our 3-year-old. In the past month or so he has begun to go ballistic whenever we talk to each other. For example, we'll be sitting at the dinner table talking about our day and he will start yelling, "No talking! Be quiet."

We send him away from the table for rudeness and then he melts down and cries in his room for half an hour. Family meals are becoming intolerable. My friends recommend a good spanking. It's a tempting idea.

A   Actually, most parents have encountered this problem at one time or another. There are two causes: First, all children think that because you have to take care of them, they possess the power to control your personal life. This false but normal belief is reinforced by a corresponding immaturity we call the "all-powerful self." To one degree or another, all children believe they have super powers. Very little ones may think they can push cars back with one hand; teens may believe that they can talk forever on the phone and get their homework done in 15 minutes.

Gentleness is the best response. When parents laugh, ridicule or become angry at children for these normal attitudes, children tend either to cling more tightly to their unrealistic beliefs or to deflate and feel helpless and powerless.

You want to try to help your 3-year-old with the upset feeling he has when you and your husband talk. Explain that mealtimes are when family members share things about their day—and that everyone needs a turn. Suggest that he go first. Then you and your husband can have a turn. If he protests, remind him that he will get another turn. Usually, this approach will work. But if he remains upset, give him a coloring book or something to do at the table while you are talking.

Unlike spankings or time-outs, this method will gently make the point that he cannot stop you and your husband from enjoying each other. It will also teach him that he can enjoy the conversation too.

How should sitter handle a demanding toddler?

Q   I'm not a parent, but I am a babysitter. I babysit a 3-year-old who melts down if I don't do what she wants.

For example, she has a wading pool and she wants me to get in it with her. When I tell her I don't want to get wet and won't fit in the pool, she tells me she hates me. When her parents get home, she tells them she doesn't like me any more. Fortunately, her parents listen when I explain what has happened. Usually, by the next time I babysit, the girl has forgotten her anger and is happy to see me. I don't know how to handle this—please help.

A   This child is in a stage where she gets much of her emotional well-being from having her caretakers respond to her requests on her terms. Her reactions are a bit more vehement than is normal, but her fragility may be increased when her parents aren't there.

The best way to respond to meltdowns is to be accepting and understanding. Say something like, "I know it's hard when I don't do what you want and you feel really angry with me, but I want to make you happy—is there something else you would like me to do?"

The best strategy is to try to avoid meltdowns altogether by using diplomacy. If you can't or don't want to do what she wants, try to give her an alternative rather than just denying her request. When she wants you to get in the wading pool, you might reply that you can't, but the ducky (or froggie or tugboat) would love to get in with her and that you and she can push it back and forth. If she wants you to play a game with her and you are occupied with something else, suggest that you will play with her as soon as possible, and in the meantime you would love to sing a song together.

If you can avoid stark negatives, you will help the girl avoid meltdowns, maintain a more positive relationship with you and develop more resilience.

How can I help my kids deal with Grandma's illness?

Q We have two children ages two and five and we have just had a big change in our family because my husband's mother, who has Parkinson's disease, has moved in with us. She has a pronounced tremor and difficulty speaking and walking. Our two-year-old son doesn't seem to notice there is anything wrong with Grandma, but our five-year-old daughter seems very upset. She wants to know what's wrong with Grandma and why the doctors can't fix it. She has become a hypochondriac and is constantly worrying that she is sick or will get sick. Sometimes she says she wishes Grandma had never come to live with us. We try to reassure her that she is fine and we tell her that we know she wouldn't really want Grandma to be taken care of by strangers, but she just sticks her chin out and says she doesn't care. Can you please advise us about the best way to handle this?

A First your five-year-old had to contend with the appearance of a younger sibling who made demands on your time, and now her grandmother needs your attention as well. So it is not surprising that she resents her grandmother's presence. She is too young to be able to feel good about caring for her grandmother because she still needs a lot of care herself. The best way to help her adjust to her grandmother's presence is to carve out time to spend alone with her doing something she enjoys. The more she feels she is getting the attention she needs from you, the less resentment she will feel. Also, if you let her know that her anger is understandable, she will feel less alienated and it will be easier for her to be affectionate with her grandmother.

As for the hypochondria, that is very normal. Children naturally copy adults. One consequence is they feel that whatever happens to important adults will happen to them. Keep reassuring your daughter that what is wrong with Grandma only happens to people who are much older than she and that most grown-ups never develop this illness at all. Over time, as she continues to be healthy, her worries about becoming like Grandma will diminish.

My 3-year-old is shy at parties

Q My 3-year-old doesn't seem to mix well with other children. When we go to a birthday party, she hangs back and doesn't participate. Other children seem to love pinning the tail on the donkey and playing duck-duck-goose, but Margery just watches from the sidelines. I ask her if she is having a good time she says, "yes," but it's hard to believe. I can't understand what is holding her back. I am worried she won't fit in at school in the fall.

A It is not uncommon for 3-year-olds in new situations to observe the scene and get their bearings. Also, many children your daughter's age are daunted by the noise and excitement of parties. Let her get comfortable in her own time.

Perhaps your daughter could use more playdates within the familiar surroundings of her own home. Then, you might introduce some of the games played at birthday parties to see if your daughter is able to enjoy them in her own home. If she can't though, just move on to an activity she is comfortable with. These shy periods are usually time-limited. And we don't think you need to worry about school. It's a few months off and teachers are usually very good at helping shy children adjust.

My child is scared of school

Q My five-year-old is starting kindergarten this fall. Previously he was in preschool for a few hours a week, but the kindergarten is all-day. When we try to talk to him about how much fun he will have in his new school he doesn't want to talk about it. Sometimes he walks out of the room or puts his hands over his ears. We also notice that he is having many more nightmares than usual and seems very easily upset during the day. We wonder if these behaviors are related to his starting school, and if so what we can do to help him since he doesn't seem to want to talk about it.

A You are correct. Your son's behavior is related to his worries about starting kindergarten. The problem is that you are trying to talk your son into looking forward to starting school by telling him how much fun he will have, rather than trying to find out what is worrying him. As a result, he feels he is doing something wrong when he can't adopt your positive attitude. So he wants to avoid all discussion of the situation.

We suggest that you change course. Tell him you recognize he has concerns about going to kindergarten and that this is normal– many children worry about starting a new school. Add that worries can be expressed in bad dreams and upset feelings. If you show your son that you are comfortable with the notion that he may be dreading school, he will probably feel more comfortable discussing his concerns. It might help to ask the librarian at your local library to suggest age-appropriate books about children who imagine that school will be unpleasant.

Once your son opens up and tells you what he fears, be careful not to contradict him ("We've met the teacher and she is very nice," or "That's silly, of course the other children will like you.") Rather, let him know how great it is that he is communicating his fears and that if anything does go wrong at school he can come right home and tell you and you will help him figure out a way to handle the problem.

Fears don't go away because someone tells you not to worry – what is reassuring is to know that if what you dread happens, you have someone to turn to who can help you. Once school starts, leave some quiet time every day – perhaps when you are putting your son to bed – to ask him how his day went. Make sure you give him an opportunity to tell you about the bad as well as the good.

Kindergarten readiness

Q Our son is going to start kindergarten this fall. He's a smart child, but he doesn't draw—he doesn't want to and can't—and barely makes legible letters. I don't want to push him, but when I compare him to his older sisters, I see that he's far behind where they were and I worry that he'll be frustrated in kindergarten, where drawing is such a big part of their day, and may get turned off to school. Would you suggest getting him tested before this becomes an issue? (I know that schools refuse to test until a child is more than a year behind grade level, so I hold out little hope for assistance from the school.)

A The most potent advice we can give you is to avoid comparing your son to his older sisters. All children develop at different rates, and while your daughters were obviously precocious with pen and paper, it is way too soon to conclude that your son has a problem.

Our guess is that the most likely explanation for his unwillingness to draw or write is that he has sensed your concern that he is not equal to his sisters in this area and has responded with a self-doubt that is inhibiting him. We suggest that you abandon all mention of drawing and writing and let your son discover the pleasure of developing these

161

skills as part of the kindergarten process. In the meantime, think of activities that he does like and do those things with him, so he can enjoy the approval from you that he so badly needs at this age.

♥

How do I handle preschool pressure?

Q My 3-year-old daughter's preschool expects her to learn her colors, numbers and letters and begin to do simple math and word recognition. My daughter is not big at sitting still and hates the worksheets. The teachers say she is falling behind.

I don't really see how a 3-year-old can be "behind," but if all the other kids are learning these things, I worry my daughter will start to feel stupid. And when I sit my daughter down and try to teach her, she puts her hands over her ears. What do you recommend?

A We increasingly hear about schools pressuring children to learn reading and math at a young age. The problem is many normal 3-, 4- and 5-year-olds are not ready to sit and do worksheets like older children. When these children fall behind, they are often put in remedial classes, even though they are normal by the older, more reasonable standard of starting reading and math in first grade. You might consider looking for a less competitive preschool.

You can also help at home. Reassure your daughter that kids learn reading and math at different ages, just as they learn to walk and talk at different times. Explain she has plenty of time to master these skills and you are confident she will.

At home, try to make learning fun. Ask how many raisins your daughter wants and then count them out for her. Leave a note on her door every day saying "I love you" and help her to read it. Ask her whether you should wear your blue shirt or your yellow shirt. When you read to her, encourage her to point out words she knows. Play car games such as finding certain words on a billboard.

Making learning fun will preserve your daughter's curiosity and enthusiasm and prepare her for school.

Little lies for no known reason

Q I have a question about lying. My six-year-old daughter tells a lot of little lies that don't seem like they have any real point. For example, she'll tell me she saw a car on the highway skid into the side of the road and the man had to get out and walk to the car place and buy a new car. She also tells some lies that have a point, like telling me she brushed her teeth when she didn't, and I understand those even though I don't like them. But how should I react when she creates these pretend stories and seems to really believe them, or at least wants me to believe them? And why does she do this?

A Your daughter is not lying—that is, she is not deliberately choosing to tell an untruth. Rather, she is behaving like a normal six-year-old and occasionally bending the truth.

Children's minds really are different from adults' minds, and one of the most significant differences is that children tend to rewrite reality to suit their emotional needs. This is a developmental phase and not a moral weakness, so there is no reason to feel upset with your daughter or to be disapproving. Most likely, her pretend stories are her way of trying to work out a recent experience that upset her; they are a form of emotional problem-solving. You neither have to agree or disagree with her words. You can just offer a comment such as, "Oh," or "That's interesting," which conveys love for your daughter and interest in what she wants to tell you without committing yourself to the truth of the story.

As your daughter gets older, she will outgrow her belief that she can change reality at will, and her creative efforts will be channeled into activities that are intended as fiction, such as short stories, plays, etc.

Why doesn't my six-year-old take responsibility for his mistakes?

Q My husband and I are very concerned about our six-year-old because when he breaks a rule or doesn't do his chores, instead of admitting his mistake and apologizing, he lies about having done it. For example, he is supposed to feed our dog every morning but sometimes he doesn't. When we confront him with it he says he put the food in but the dog ate all of it. We know this isn't true.

We have tried to explain to him the importance of admitting mistakes and why it is bad to lie, but he continues to insist he didn't do anything wrong. We are at a loss what to do next.

A The problem is not that your son is "lying," but that you are expecting behavior that is way beyond your son's years. Bending the truth is normal behavior at this age, especially when a child fears that something he has done will have unpleasant consequences. Moreover, children this age are not ready to be autonomously reliable about chores or rules that seem burdensome.

The irony is that the more critical you are of your child when he makes a mistake, the more he will be driven to deny that he has done anything wrong and the longer it will take him to become a person who takes responsibility for his actions. On the other hand, if you adjust your expectations to fit your son's level of maturity, you will find it easier to remain good humored when your son makes an error, with the result that he will not have to resort to denial.

For example, if he forgets to feed the dog, rather than criticizing him for what is really an age-appropriate lapse, you might say in a friendly way, "Looks like you got busy and forgot to feed Henry. I'll hold the bowl for you if you'll pour the food in." If you respond with this kind of understanding and offer a helping hand, your son will not be driven to deny reality in an attempt to avoid the pain caused when his beloved parents disapprove of him.

When to tell kids the truth

Q What is the role of "white lies" in parenting? I'm always telling my children—six-year-old twins—to be honest and truthful, but when their hamster died, I told them she ran away. This got me thinking about other lies I've told them, like when I've thrown out something that belongs to them while cleaning their room, thinking that they wouldn't notice, and then they ask where it is and I say, "I don't know." Or when they ask if I'll buy them an ice cream cone at the swimming pool and I say, "I don't have any money on me." I'm trying to be gentle on their feelings and avoid unnecessary arguments, but is this a good way to deal with these kinds of things?

A The issue of when to tell white lies to children is complex. Certainly, there are facts from which children need to be protected. In general, it is helpful to try to protect children from the truth when they are too young to understand it but old enough to be really upset by it. For example, you should try to shield a three-year-old from knowing all the risks of a surgery you have to undergo.

In the examples you give, though, your children are aware that a loss has occurred (their hamster is gone, they can't have ice cream, they can't find their toy), so it is not a question of whether or not to tell your children about something unpleasant. The question is, what is the best way to help them with a disappointment they are already feeling? The answer is that when parents try to protect children by preventing them from feeling anger and sadness, children remain confused, upset, and without a place to turn.

Telling the children that their hamster ran away doesn't keep them from missing their pet. Instead of the unhappiness of knowing their hamster is dead, the children have the equally painful feelings of believing the hamster didn't like living with them and of uncertainty about where the hamster has gone. What children really need to cope with the loss of a pet is parents' willingness to hear and to respond sympathetically to their upset feelings. If you tell children the truth, they will feel very sad, but they will also learn that they can turn to you for comfort and that the death of a loved one does not have to be devastating.

When you tell your children that you don't have money for ice cream, you imply that you would have bought them ice cream if you had the money. But eventually your children will figure out that in fact you don't want them to have sweets at that time. It would be more helpful to explain that they can't have ice cream now, but they can have some after dinner. Your children would learn that they can't always have what they want when they want it, but they have you to help them have what they want in a way that is healthy for them.

If you tell your children you don't know what happened to a toy they still want, they will feel that there are mysterious and malevolent forces loose in their home, or they will blame themselves for losing the toy and search for it in vain. If you admit that you threw the toy out believing that they didn't want it any longer, you can apologize and work out a better system for choosing old toys to discard. Your children will learn that you can recognize, admit, and learn from mistakes and they will feel more comfortable with the mistakes they make.

So next time something goes wrong in your children's lives, try to face the problem directly with them and offer a caring ear for their upset feelings. This approach will teach your children the most important lesson of all, which is that no matter what disappointments life brings them, your love and affection remain steady and reliable.

It's time to come clean about your "story"

Q My five-year-old son was afraid of the water when he was 2½. We took him to a swim class and the instructor told him that once he learned to swim by himself really well, Willy, the whale in the movie "Free Willy," would come and swim with him.

I don't know what got into us, but we went along with this story and continued to promise that Willy would join him when he learned to swim.

Now, of course, our lie has caught up with us. My son can swim and asks us every day when Willy is coming. So our question is, "Now what?" Do we admit the lie and disappoint him? Do we continue to perpetuate this myth, or do we make up something like, "Willy actually was let loose and no one knows where he is now"? If we do tell him we lied, how do we explain why we lied, and how will he understand when we get after him for lying?

Please don't tell us we shouldn't have gotten ourselves into this—we know that now. The question is, how do we get out of it?

A We think the best thing is to end the subterfuge and tell your son that you made a mistake in going along with the swim teacher's story about Willy. Explain that you were trying to help him to get past his fear of water, but that you can see now that promising him something that couldn't happen was not really fair.

Perhaps you might see if you can find a stuffed animal that looks like Willy and tell your son that you know he was expecting the real thing, but since you can't deliver on that promise, you hope he will accept the toy Willy as part of your apology.

If you try to perpetuate the made-up story in any form, your son will eventually become mature enough to understand the truth. At that point he will feel even worse because more time will have passed and more "stories" will have been told to him.

Better to get this behind you and move on.

Are my kids too materialistic?

Q This year I was really struck by how important presents were to my kids (ages three and six) at Christmas. It seemed like they were mainly interested in what they were getting, not in the parts of the holiday that matter most to me. We've tried to encourage them to get into the story of Christmas, the religious meaning, as well as the beauty and the family togetherness, but they seem to be focused mainly on the presents. I'm sure we'll encounter the same thing at birthdays and next year at Christmas. Any advice?

A Like many parents, you are frustrated with your children for not acting more grown up. Yet the reality is that they lack the ability to meet your expectations. The reason is that at this point, their minds are nothing like the mind of an adult.

It is normal and natural for your children to focus on the fun of getting presents and not be terribly interested in the more abstract meanings of Christmas that are important to you. Their intense interest in gifts does not mean that they will grow up materialistic or unable to appreciate the religious or family significance of Christmas.

It is so important to remember that children are works in progress and that the way they are at three and six is not a sign of how they will be at twenty-three or twenty-six (or even at thirteen and sixteen). As your children's minds mature, abstractions such as religion or family togetherness will become real and meaningful to them. So rather than feeling disappointed in your children, you can be proud of them for developing normally. Paradoxically, the best way to teach them to appreciate family togetherness and religious values is simply to love and enjoy them; they will copy your caring and compassion and become the adults you are hoping for.

Do piano lessons have to be a daily battle?

Q I need your advice about how to deal with my six-year-old son who wanted piano lessons but doesn't want to practice. His piano teacher says he should practice at least two minutes a day. When I remind him, he says, "In a minute, Mom." But a minute drags on and on and he never gets to it. Then I tell him that he either has to practice or he can't watch TV or play video games. He gets mad and slams the door to his room. Once in a while, he will sit down at the piano and spend about a minute playing before he stops and says he has practiced. When he keeps playing, he asks me every two seconds how long is left. This clearly isn't working, but I don't know what to do. He likes his piano teacher and says he doesn't want to stop taking lessons, but this conflict over practicing is making me crazy. How can I get him to practice without so much unpleasantness?

A Fighting with your son over practicing is not going to achieve your aim of helping him enjoy music. Unlike school homework, piano practicing is optional. If he doesn't like practicing piano, there are lots of other instruments your son might prefer. Or, perhaps he is more interested in art or sports. We can't overemphasize that extracurricular activities should add pleasure, not conflict, to life. So take a deep breath and tell your son that if he doesn't want to practice, you will help him find another activity he will like better.

♥

My 3-year-old reader won't read when we request it

Q My 3-year-old has amazed her father and me by learning to read by herself (with a little help from "Sesame Street"). She can read chapter books. We are so proud that we often ask her to show our friends and relatives. I would think she would enjoy the admiration, but she has begun to refuse to read when asked. Now I find that she doesn't want to read to her father and me anymore. I don't understand this behavior and don't know what to do. Should we insist that she read since we know she can? Please advise.

A It is wonderful that you have a child who enjoys reading enough to teach herself how to do it. However, like all children her age, she resists doing thing (even things she likes) on command. Reading out loud was fine as long as it was her idea, but once it became a requirement, the fun went out of it for her. Because reading will be such an important part of the rest of your daughter's life, you want to act quickly to preserve it as a source of pleasure for her. We suggest that for the time being you "forget" that she can read. Don't mention this ability to anyone, don't ask her to read to others or yourselves, and go back to reading to her. Once she realizes that the pressure is off, she may begin to read words or sentences again. Simply say, "Good job!" and continue reading to her. In other words, remove reading from the sphere of conflict and let it be entirely her choice once again. Then your daughter will reconnect with the enjoyment she first felt from reading and she will be back on track for success at school and in life.

Ending nightmares requires comfort

Q My five-year-old has always had nightmares, but they seem to be getting worse. He comes running into our bedroom screaming and crying, too frightened to go back to bed by himself. Last night, he dreamed aliens were taking over the world. He went to his Dad for help only to discover Dad was an alien.

My husband tells him to stop being such a baby and get back to bed. But my son is really frightened. So, I usually sit with him while he gets back to sleep. Often, he wakes up again and everything is repeated. Because my husband won't help, I am not getting enough sleep. My husband thinks I am being overindulgent. What do you think?

A People are the authors of their own dreams. So your son is creating nightmares as a way of trying to cope with troubling daytime feelings or events. He is not choosing to have nightmares, but the explanation is in his waking life. Perhaps, the child is made to feel ashamed of angry feelings. Or he is often punished or yelled at. In school-age children, it can result from being bullied at school or day care. In other cases, the nightmares are linked to parents who argue or who are physically or emotionally unavailable to the child.

Your son is in a developmental stage called the Romantic Phase. He wants all your attention and sees his father as a rival. Like all little boys, he worries that his Dad will become aware of his competitive feelings and retaliate. So when your husband becomes irritated at his fright and calls him a baby, it heightens your son's fears, which is probably why he dreamed that about his father. Explain to your husband his negative reactions are not helping. Also, try to convince your husband your son needs to be soothed, not ridiculed. You are right to comfort your son. The more kindness he receives, the fewer nightmares he is likely to have.

Terrifying nightmares

Q We read with concern the recent article in Chicago Parent by Mary Carr about sleep terrors. Our concern is that our son, too, has sleep terrors. He is six years old and seems to be doing OK with his friends, although his teacher says that he is not working at his capacity at school. He has had sleep terrors for two years and our neighbor, who is a pediatric nurse, says not to worry—that he will grow out of them. We can do nothing to comfort him when these terrors occur and, as Ms. Carr said, he seems to forget them in the morning.

While Ms. Carr says there is no treatment for sleep terrors, my wife's uncle, who is a clinical social worker, says that this is a very serious emotional problem and that our son needs help. We don't want to take him to a therapist needlessly. Thank you for helping us with this difficult problem.

A You are right to be concerned about your son's sleep terrors. While any child can have a terrifying nightmare once in a while, a child who has had sleep terrors for two years could definitely benefit from professional help.

All dreams are written and produced by the dreamer. The fact that your son has an ongoing need to create dreams that frighten him half to death is a sign that he has many fears and a tremendous amount of anger at himself and others that he cannot get a handle on during the day.

We know from many years of clinical experience that it is categorically untrue that there is no help for night terrors. As a parent, being as positive and gentle with your son as possible will give him a model of treating himself and others with compassion rather than anger. Also think through his day with the aim of reducing conflict and times when he may feel inadequate. For example, perhaps he is participating in an extracurricular activity that is more of a struggle than a pleasure. If so, suggest that he might want to discontinue the stressful activity for a while and free up some unstructured time.

Perhaps there are stresses in your family, such as marital conflict or a serious illness. Children often blame themselves when things go wrong, and may attempt to come to terms with their fears and anger in their dreams.

If, in spite of your efforts to make your son's day more enjoyable and less stressful, the night terrors continue, take him to a professional with special training in the psychological treatment of children. The therapeutic relationship will be able to help him with his angry, fearful feelings during the day, so that he won't need to struggle with them so dramatically at night.

How can I help calm my son's fears?

Q My 5-year-old son has become very fearful. He worries about terrorist attacks, that my husband and I will get in an accident, that he will be kidnapped or that his dog will die. He is in a new school (kindergarten) and seems OK there, although he doesn't seem to have made many friends. He wanted to go to the kindergarten his friends go to, but we moved out of that district, and this new school is better. My husband is impatient with our son and feels that he is acting like a sissy. I find his behavior irritating, but would like to understand it better. Can you help?

A We believe your son's fears are caused by angry feelings over the move and change of schools. Young children have a very unrealistic belief in the power of their anger—they think that the strength of the anger they feel is an indication of the effect it will have on the outside world. If your son is angry at you for forcing him to leave his friends, he may experience this anger as so powerful that he is worried about your safety. He may also worry that you will retaliate for his destructive wishes, which explains his concerns for his own safety and for his dog. Tell him that you imagine that he may have a lot of upset feelings about the move. Explain that you may not have paid enough attention to his sadness at leaving his friends, his neighborhood and his school behind. Encourage him to talk about those feelings and make it possible for him to visit his old neighborhood and friends. You might also explain that these angry feelings won't cause harm to come to those he is angry with. And please tell your husband that your son is not a "sissy"—children's fears can be overwhelming to them.

How can I help my toddler better express her feelings?

Q My 3-year-old daughter makes her likes and dislikes clearly known. Generally, I'm glad she's assertive—except when she states, often loudly, that she doesn't like her two grandmothers. These women tend to be judgmental and easily hurt. They wind up glaring at me, while I try to explain to my daughter that saying, "I don't like Grandma," hurts Grandma's feelings.

My ex-husband believes she should be nice to these people and punishes with a "time out" if she is not. I value her ability to be authentic, but also realize she needs to learn not to hurt others' feelings. The other day it happened when her father came to pick her up to bring to his house and she didn't want to go. She cried for a while after he turned off the television and said she needed to get going. My ex said I was rewarding her by holding her and not being more firm in making her go with him right away. Any suggestions?

A We suggest you stick to your guns. The grandmothers and your ex-husband are expecting way too much of a 3-year-old. Given your description of the grandmothers as judgmental and overly sensitive, it is not surprising they are not your daughter's favorite people.

Your daughter is much too young to be told to pretend to be nice to people she doesn't like. This will only confuse her and teach her there is something wrong with ever feeling negatively about someone. In later years, this may make it difficult for her to avoid abusive relationships and to choose positive, caring friends and partners.

Talk to your daughter about the fact that while you understand that she sometimes has negative feelings about her grandmothers, it would be better if she talked to you about these feelings in private rather than discussing them with her grandmothers. If she does make a negative comment, she should not be punished. As she gets older, she will naturally become more aware of what others are feeling, and she will then be much more inclined to keep her negative opinions to herself.

Your ex-husband, meanwhile, needs to understand that transitions are difficult for young children, particularly children whose parents are divorced. Your daughter used to have both parents at once and now is with only one at a time, so it is not surprising that it is difficult for her to leave you and go with her father. If your ex can be helped to recognize this, then perhaps he could be more gentle and understanding with your daughter. For example, he could talk about the fun things they are going to do together and that although he knows it's hard to leave Mom, she may call you during their visit. The more kindness he shows her at these difficult moments, the more positively your daughter will feel about her visits with him.

Handling calls to 911

Q My six-year-old daughter recently called 911 when I was not in the room and then hung up, prompting the emergency operator to call back and ask if there was a problem. I realized she knew she had done something wrong because she got nervous when the phone rang again. My first instinct was to chastise her for the prank call, but I held back, concerned that she might be afraid to ever call that number again, even when she needs to. We talked about it afterwards and went over the right and wrong reasons for calling, but I'm afraid she might have been spooked. Any thoughts on how I should have handled this?

A As far as it went, your response was excellent. It was certainly wise not to be so negative that your daughter would hesitate to call 911 in a real emergency.

We would suggest, though, that you consider another dimension to her action. Perhaps she was trying to get help with a problem that is bothering her but that for some reason she is afraid to discuss with you. Children are told so often that 911 is the place to go for assistance, that maybe your daughter was hoping she could have a heart-to-heart with the operator. Try to talk to her about whether there was something upsetting her when she made the call. You might even have an inkling of what was bothering her, such as problems with siblings or friends. Often children who are having an unpleasant time with other adults (such as a babysitter, a friend's parent, or even a close relative) are afraid to mention this to their parents.

Most important, though, is to emphasize that no matter what is troubling your daughter, you are her personal 911 and that, like the operator, you are on call 24 hours a day to hear her troubles. When she does confide in you, be sure to show her that you take her concerns seriously and that you welcome her confidence.

The importance of a shared surname

Q "So what's your name?" That's a question that brings my four-year-old son to tears. My son in his heart believes that his last name is the same as mine. His father and I were never married, however, my son has his father's last name. In addition, my son does not know his father. (His father's choice.) When I tried to correct him and tell him his legal name he cries. He lost about two weeks of sleep because of this.

For two years people have been tiptoeing around his name. I

want to legally change his last name to mine. Is this the right thing to do for my son's emotional stability? I really need some professional advice. Thank you!

A You are right to think that it will be tremendously helpful to your son to give him your last name. You are the person who has loved him, fed him, dried his tears, and been there for him in good times and bad. You are the person whose love makes him feel good about himself and inspires him to be caring and compassionate to others. It is natural and healthy for him to want to be as much like you as possible, including having your name.

In contrast, every time your son is called or calls himself by his father's name, he is reminded that his father, who should be, like you, a source of love and caring, is choosing to be unavailable. His father's name evokes painful feelings of not being appealing enough to make his father love him and presents him with a model of a parent who is unreachable and uncaring.

Changing your son's name will benefit both of you, because it will reflect the true state of affairs: that you are your son's real parent and role model and will cement the bond between you that your love and dedication have forged over the last four years.

Expressing parental anger

Q I haven't yet read your book, *Smart Love*, but I am eager to do so. The disciplining of children in a compassionate way is something I strive for everyday, and I'm looking forward to gaining new insight from your book.

We have two beautiful sons, ages six and two, who are spirited and strong-willed. My husband and I are very intense and show our emotions with a lot of passion. We are a loving family, but many times seem to find it difficult to stay calm, not yell, and find an intelligent way to deal with misbehavior. Especially at the dinner hour or at times when we would really like to get something accomplished without interruption.

Is there a compassionate way to express anger? I've thought long and hard about this, and know that having angry and discouraging feelings toward my children is realistic. What do I do with the moments when I seem to have nothing left and want to be in control, but let my emotions get the best of me?

A It is certainly true that all parents get angry and exasperated with their children at times, and it is admirable that you are striving to find the most constructive way to handle your anger. We have found that the best way for parents to keep their anger from having a negative impact on their children's emotional development is to avoid holding their children responsible for their angry feelings.

We know that parents are often told that it is good for children to know that their behavior has made their parents angry. But when parents behave angrily toward children, children's love of their parents drives them to copy them. Over time, children will learn to use anger and self-rejection as a way of managing themselves and as a response to others with whom they disagree.

Usually parents feel angry at their children for one of two reasons: the parents themselves have had a bad day or feel exhausted and depleted, or the parents are expecting their children to act more grown up than they really are. In either case, the best response is to take a deep breath, go in another room for a moment if necessary to compose yourself, and try to avoid communicating that anger to your children. You will make a tremendous contribution to your children's future well-being if you avoid making them feel responsible for your anger.

If in spite of your good intentions you do blow up, you can neutralize the effect on your children with a straightforward apology.

You might say, "I'm sorry I got angry at you. I never want to yell at you."

You mention that you feel particularly angry when your children are difficult at dinner or when you need uninterrupted time. But two-year-olds and even six-year-olds are too young to meet standards of adult etiquette. They find it difficult to sit quietly at dinner and to wait patiently for their parents' attention. So the behavior that is making you angry is actually quite normal. We suggest that you work on projects that require your undivided attention only after the boys are asleep or at times when your husband can watch the boys, and that you adjust your expectations for the dinner hour to allow the boys room to be boys. Perhaps you and your husband can recharge your parenting batteries by finding time to have an occasional adult dinner alone.

How do I handle kids with different personalities?

Q I am interested in your viewpoint about how to respond to siblings with different personalities. I have two boys, ages one and four. From birth, they were totally different. The four-year-old is high strung, sensitive and easily upset. The one-year-old is resilient and laughs off most things. Because he is so easygoing, it is very easy to parent him.

I feel like my four-year-old needs to learn to be tougher to cope with life, but I am not sure how to help him. We try telling him that he is upset over nothing and acting like more of a baby than his little brother, but then he gets mad. My friend told me to ignore his tears unless they are for a "good reason," but that doesn't feel right to me.

A There is no conclusive scientific evidence that personality is inborn. The preponderance of evidence suggests the opposite is true—personality can be responsive to ongoing life experience.

Keep in mind that every newborn has been affected by nine months of prenatal experience. Increasingly, research shows how formative those months are. Babies are born able to recognize their mother's voice, to know which stories were read to them in utero and to recognize their native language.

Also, babies born to mothers who have experienced significant stress during pregnancy are more likely to produce greater than average amounts of stress hormones themselves and to be harder to soothe than other babies.

Babies' personalities are not fixed—they can change. You can help your older boy become calmer and more resilient. The way to make him happier is by recognizing and accounting for his sensitivities—not by following your friend's advice and ignoring those sensitivities.

We suggest that you notice what causes your son to fall apart and try to eliminate or anticipate those occasions. For example, if he becomes upset when you pay attention to his brother, find something fun for him to do beforehand.

When he does cry, open your arms and your heart to him. Like adults, children appreciate the opportunity to turn to a warm relationship when they are unhappy. Once your son knows that he can come to you for help when he is upset, his inner sense of well-being will be more stable. The result will be that he will be more flexible and less volatile.

Should I allow my five-year-old to play with a toy water gun?

Q Would you please describe your stance on toy gun play for children? I just recently relented and bought a toy water gun for my five-year-old, and am not sure I should have. I find all the associated noises, "bang, bang, you're dead" unnerving, and could use some help in guiding his play. What is the research regarding this? What is your spin? Thanks!

A There is convincing research showing that children who have problems with aggression are made more aggressive by violent movies, TV programs and video games. Giving these children toy guns may also stimulate their aggression. But if your son is not inclined to frequent angry outbursts, hitting or biting, giving him a water gun is unlikely to harm him. When he says "bang, bang, you're dead" he is engaging in fantasy play that is not very different from pretending to be a monster who eats people or any of the other aggressive fantasies young children sometimes act out. You don't need to intervene in this play any more than you would stop him from fantasy play about goblins or witches.

On the other hand, if your son begins to hit people or animals with the gun, or you notice that in general he is becoming much more aggressive, restrict the water gun to bath time and don't buy him other toy weapons. If he tends to focus his gunplay on pointing the gun at you and saying he is going to kill you, it is very important to reassure him that his anger will not destroy you or make you disappear. Tell him that you love him and will continue to be there for him even when he is feeling angry. Then ask him if he knows what he is angry about and tell him that letting you know about these feelings will not hurt you but will make it possible for you to help him feel better. This will be much more constructive than focusing on the gun itself. After all, he can also pretend to shoot you with a block or a finger.

Discouraging gun play

Q My husband and I feel strongly about not exposing our four-year-old son to violence and toy guns. He only watches PBS programs and Disney movies, which we realize do unfortunately contain some violence. For some reason, however, he is enamored with guns and swords.

We do not have guns in our house and have made it clear guns are dangerous weapons that hurt people and are not to be played with. Even though he doesn't own any toy guns, he uses anything remotely resembling a gun to pretend to shoot, usually into the air or to get "the bad guys." (He takes apart his car track and uses the pieces of road way or rips paper into gun shapes.) Otherwise, he's a happy, seemingly well-adjusted kid. At times, I wonder if our rules against guns make them more interesting to him and whether we should just let him play out this phase of his fantasy life. Thank you for your consideration of this issue.

A We think you hit the nail on the head when you suggest that your rules against guns have backfired and made guns seem more attractive to your son. Because children are natural imitators, it is a good idea to shield youngsters from programs with violent content. At the same time preschoolers are too young to understand lectures about the danger of guns (just as they are too young to be reliable about staying out of the street and away from hot stoves). Moreover, children your son's age are naturally inclined to resist being told what to do.

So the power struggle you find yourself in with your son follows from your repeated attempts to warn him away from guns. We suggest that you drop all discussion of the dangers of guns and of his pretend use of them. If he is pretending to shoot a gun, just make a mild comment such as, "Yes, I see." After a few minutes, gently suggest another activity. Once your son has nothing to struggle against, the gun play will most likely decrease substantially.

You don't mention whether your son is in preschool, but if he is, he also may be copying the gun play from other children there. Most important is to realize that it is natural for him to want to be like other children his age and that playing with guns now is not a sign that he will want to have anything to do with real guns when he grows up. The best way to ensure that your son will not turn to violent means to settle disputes as an adult is to offer lots of love, affection and respect during his formative years. With that model, your son will use words not weapons to handle adult disagreements.

Kids who hate to lose at games

Q My four-year-old son has a lot of trouble not being the winner or not being perfect at games and sports of all kinds. He loves winning (being first in a race, getting to move ahead in a game, etc.) When he doesn't win (comes in second, misses a turn, drops a catch) he pouts, yells, quits, or cries.

This includes very low-key competition and general play, when winning isn't a goal (at least to others involved). He is cared for by adults who aren't very competitive by nature, and certainly aren't encouraging a win/lose mentality. Talking with him during and after games about this hasn't proven helpful. Is this developmentally predictable? Can you suggest how my husband and I can help him?

A Your son's upset at losing is normal behavior not only for four-year-olds but for older children as well. All children derive much of their everyday happiness from getting what they want when they want it.

The process by which children learn that they can enjoy playing a game they don't win is a gradual one that isn't completed until adolescence. The best way to help your son grow up to be an adult who can enjoy a good effort whether or not it results in a win is to avoid lecturing him now and to be sympathetic when he melts down. You might say something like, "I know you're upset and disappointed. This game seems to be making you unhappy. Would you like to do something else, like take a walk or have me read you a story?"

By sympathizing with his upset feelings and helping him find a more enjoyable activity, you help your son to learn that while he cannot always count on winning, he can always count on your love and support. The fundamental certainty that he is always loved and loveable will enable him to become a person who can lose a game without losing his inner equilibrium and who, as a result, will be able to enjoy playing a game he doesn't win.

No one wins all the time

Q I am a home daycare provider with six children in my care. This summer, my program is overwhelmingly full of boys, and some new issues have come up.

One of the boys currently at my home, who is five years old, has the hardest time when playing games if he is not the one always ahead and the winner. He wants to play an organized game such as football, baseball, dinosaur checkers, etc., but he storms off if anyone gets slightly ahead of him. I explain that one of the boys is almost two years older than him and therefore has had two years more experience than he has. The other boys, who range in age from four to six, back me up with this and try to help me explain this to the boy. The other kids tell him, "No one wins all of the time." But he gets so upset and quits the game and vows never to come back here. What do you suggest we say or do to help him?

A This is a striking example of a child with a strong appetite for competitive games that is powered not by love of playing but by a desperate need to succeed. As a result, he must win in order to feel worthwhile. Losing, or even falling behind, confirms all his fears of being inadequate and causes him to feel unbearable pain. It is no wonder, then, that his response to this misery is the wish to leave and not come back.

Because he is not in control of this vicious circle, efforts to get him to consider the inevitability of defeat are doomed to fail. And even when he wins, his relief will be short-lived as his underlying insecurity continues unabated, and the specter of losing continues to loom on his horizon.

The kindest and most helpful thing to do for this child is to encourage him to pursue activities that are consistently enjoyable and allow him to feel in control of a successful outcome. Activities that would be good for this boy would be non-competitive. We suggest that you tell him in a friendly and non-judgmental manner that for now you are going to find something else for him to do when the other children are playing sports. Explain that since his response to losing is to feel terrible about himself, it would be better not to play these games until he can feel comfortable inside when he doesn't win. Because you are helping him and not punishing him, do try to find a noncompetitive substitute activity that he will truly enjoy, such as painting or building.

We would emphasize that since this child's central problem is his insecurity, he may react even to non-competitive activities by feeling inadequate. For example, he may say that the picture he painted "stinks." However, it will be easier to help him feel good about his effort in a context where there are not clear winners and losers. In general, the greatest gift you can give this boy is to relate to him in a manner that tells him he is likeable, liked just for himself, and respected as a capable, competent person. In this way, you will make a real contribution to his future emotional well-being.

Putting up with potty talk

Q I have three boys, ages six, four and two. Recently, my two oldest boys have been having fun laughing at words like poop, pee, toot, tush, etc. This is especially true when their friends come over. Then they all chime in.

I encourage them to use their good words and try to be funny a different way. I understand that this is a phase they go through, but was wondering how I should approach it. Should I try to ignore it or censor it, or fall somewhere in the middle?

A This is a perfect example of normal behavior that will be outgrown if you don't focus on it and disapprove of it, but that will persist long after it would otherwise be left behind if you make an issue of it. Many children, especially boys the ages of your sons, think that bathroom humor is hilarious. Consider the popularity of the *Captain Underpants* series!

The words your boys are using are not "bad," although they certainly sound juvenile and not particularly funny to grownups. If you disapprove of these words, you will cause your boys to become defensive and cling to them, or to feel ashamed and naughty. Either way, you will be giving them the message that they are doing something wrong when in reality they are behaving normally for their ages. Practice a tolerant smile, and try not to reprimand your boys for behavior that is both harmless and age-appropriate.

The preschool and potty training dilemma

Q My daughter is 3 and will start preschool this fall. We don't know what to do because the preschool requires that kids be toilet trained, and she still wears pull-ups and shows no interest in using the potty. She tried the potty a few months ago, but didn't like it. Now she just shakes head head "no" when we ask her. Sometimes if we offer her a reward she will use the potty, but only for that time. I know she would like preschool, but I don't know how to get her potty trained.

A We have known many 3- and 4-year-olds who resisted using the potty in general but who were willing to use it for specific periods to participate in an activity of their choice, such as school or swimming lessons. If your daughter likes the idea of preschool, most likely she will be willing to use the potty to attend. Describe the fun she will have at preschool, focusing on the activities you think she would like most. Then explain to her that at school she needs to use the potty like the other children. Let her know she can keep her pull-ups the rest of the day. Since your daughter will use the potty to get a reward of your choosing, she will probably use it to attain a goal of her own choosing. On the other hand, if preschool doesn't appeal to her, it's unlikely she will accept the notion of using the potty there, and you may have to wait one more year.

Helping my daughter with preschool fears

Q Our four-year-old daughter is a very happy and well-loved child. She chose to use the toilet at age two and has had few accidents, all of which have been handled gently with a "no big deal" attitude. After attending a wonderful preschool for about six months, she had an accident and wet her pants. She says she didn't go to the bathroom because she didn't want to miss snack. Now she doesn't want to go back to school. The nights before school she gets so upset and anxious she cries and refuses to go to school unless I go with her. When we go, she loves being there, but when we talk about her going to school on her own she gets upset and tells me she'll miss me too much. This is unusual since she's never been insecure about my temporary absence.

Knowing it is related to the accident, I ask her what upset her the most about it. She says, "I was embarrassed." I tell her it is normal to have accidents and that many people, including adults, have them. I tell her she can wear Pull-Ups if that would help. "No way" is her response. The school has been very helpful and understanding, but I can't keep going with her forever. Please help me to help her return to her well-adjusted, happy childhood.

A Our hunch is that your daughter is putting her finger on the problem when she says she felt embarrassed by wetting her pants. Either the teachers weren't as supportive as you think, or she was teased by other children. When you are there with her, she feels that if she were to wet herself again she would be protected from painful feelings. We suggest you check with the school to make sure children aren't being allowed to tease others who make mistakes. Perhaps you also could send an extra set of clothes and underclothes so she will not worry about having to stay in wet clothes in case of another accident.

Meanwhile, tell your daughter you will continue to go to school with her as long as she needs you. When she seems more relaxed, try leaving for a few minutes every day. If she does well in your absence, gradually increase the time you are gone. Eventually, she will be able to go to school by herself again. Most important is to take her fear seriously whether it makes sense to you or not. If you can give her this leeway now, chances are you will avoid school problems later on.

💜

Ready for Preschool

Q How do you know when to enroll your child into preschool? Do you feel preschool is a necessity or a luxury? Our almost four-year-old was enrolled in a preschool last year but we pulled him out after two weeks due to what we believed was poor timing and separation anxiety. (Poor timing being, birth of second child, a good friend and neighbor moved away, and our son was still not completely potty trained.) Our son is extremely shy and timid. He relates best to people on a one-to-one basis or very small group. He is overwhelmed by larger groups. While we know socialization would be best for him, we feel we may be pressuring him to do something he is not yet comfortable with. We also don't believe his shyness is a phase he will grow out of, but that this is who he is; that his shyness is part of his disposition. What do you suggest?

A You did exactly the right thing when you responded to your son's unhappiness at preschool by deciding to wait another year. We suggest the following guidelines for knowing whether children are ready for preschool: they are comfortable separating from parents for short periods of time (they are happy to go to a friend's house to play, they like to go with a relative to the playground); they usually enjoy being in the company of other children; they have chosen to use the toilet; they can sit quietly and work on a project for twenty minutes at a time; and they are generally willing to follow directions. Since the goal is not to force your little boy into accepting separation but to help him develop a positive attitude toward school, it was wise not to leave him before he felt ready to separate.

The presence of a new sibling who gets to stay close to home and to parents during the day can make older siblings feel an intense need for parental love and attention. As a result, the arrival of a new sibling may have undermined whatever readiness for school your son may have been feeling.

We cannot emphasize too much that when your son starts school is much less important than how he feels when he is there. Because this will be his first introduction to school, you are so right to do everything you can to ensure that he will enjoy it. The true object of preschool is not to teach your son specific facts (letters, numbers), but to teach him to like school and to feel happy and competent there. If this goal is met, he will enter grammar school with optimism and self-confidence.

Since your son is uncomfortable with large groups, maybe you could find a preschool in your area with small classes. But if he still doesn't seem ready this fall, we suggest that you avoid forcing the issue. There are many enjoyable activities you could do with your son this year (visit museums, go together to music, pottery or gymnastic classes, etc.). By the time he starts kindergarten, he will certainly be more confident and ready to make the most of the school experience.

How can I help my 3-year-old adjust to moving?

Q My husband and I recently relocated here from Texas. In the weeks before the move, my 3-year-old was easily upset and cried a lot. I realized she was reacting to the move and I tried to be understanding. I thought once we were in the new house and she started a new preschool and met new friends, she would be fine. But her disposition is worse than before—she tells my husband

and me that she hates us and melts down if she can't have what she wants immediately. Suggestions?

A Moving can be very disruptive for children who had no part in the decision. No matter how carefully adults explain their reasons for moving, young children cannot relate to adult logic and feel they are arbitrarily being torn from friends and familiar surroundings. They become angry with the people responsible for their upset—their parents.

These are age-appropriate reactions—not signs children are spoiled or egocentric. We suggest you try to be especially patient during this adjustment period. If she always says she hates you, tell her that you know that she didn't want to move and you can understand that she feels angry about it. If she melts down over nothing, reassure her that you know things feel harder than before because she is still getting used to the new place.

Parents often want children to be happy in the new house and to appreciate how much trouble parents took to make the move easier. But before children can begin to enjoy their new surroundings, they need some time to express their feeling of having lost their old way of life. If you are accepting of your daughter's upset, you will actually accelerate her adjustment to her new life.

♥

How private should parents be?

Q At what age (or stage) should parents be careful that their children don't see them naked, particularly children of the opposite gender? And is there any general wisdom about when parents should teach children to be more private about their own bodies?

A   This is one of those issues that is to some extent culture specific, so we emphasize that we are limiting the scope of our answer to our own culture.

It is not necessary for parents of the same sex as the child to conceal their nakedness from the child in appropriate contexts, such as changing clothes or showering. In our culture children will grow up seeing members of their own sex naked in locker rooms, camp cabins, the military, etc. Children would be confused and potentially made uncomfortable later if the same-sex parent went to great lengths never to be seen naked by the child.

Parents do need to be prepared to answer questions such as, "Why don't I have breasts like yours?" The best answers are simple and matter-of-fact. "You will when you grow up. You'll grow up to look just like me."

On the other hand, we recommend that children over three be spared from seeing the opposite-sex parent naked or both parents naked together. The child at this age is entering what we call the romantic phase. The child realizes that although the parents love and care for the child, the parents also have a special and enjoyable relationship that excludes the child. The child reacts to this perception by wanting the special attention the opposite-sex parent bestows on the same-sex parent. When the child fails to attract the opposite-sex parent's social attention, the child blames the same-sex parent and then becomes concerned that the same-sex parent will perceive this anger and retaliate.

This is an emotionally charged time in development, and seeing the opposite-sex parent naked will be very overstimulating and make it more difficult for the child to accomplish the developmental task at hand: to accept the child's role in the family, which means accepting that the child will never get the same social attention from the opposite-sex parent that the same-sex parent enjoys.

As to your second question, children younger than three can not understand the notion that parts of their body are private and should be off-limits to others any more than they can really grasp that cars can hurt them or electrical outlets can shock them. Children over three can understand that their body has private parts and that it is important to tell their parents if anyone tries to touch them there.

TV news too scary for sensitive youngsters

Q I need help deciding what to let my five-year-old watch on TV. My husband and I were watching the news this week and there was coverage of an airplane crash that killed two people. They showed the smoking wreckage and talked about how no one lived and they have no idea what happened. We are scheduled to visit my parents on the East Coast in a couple of weeks and now my son is having nightmares and says he doesn't want to fly. Should we have shielded him from the news? My husband argues you can't protect your children from "real life" and he just has to learn that bad things happen. What is your opinion? And how can we convince him to get on the plane?

A How much television news children should be exposed to depends both on their age and their psychological makeup. Children as young as your son have great difficulty distancing themselves from crimes and disasters. If they see a hit-and-run or a murder scene on TV, they typically feel the same horrible fate is about to happen to them. They may become visibly upset immediately, they may have nightmares or they may inhibit their activities in the hope of avoiding a similar fate (refusing to fly, for example). Each of these reactions indicates that seeing the news was overwhelming to the child and that the child needs to be shielded from similar news programs until he is older.

Children older than eight vary considerably in their reaction to sad events. Some are able to feel compassion for the people affected without becoming fearful themselves. But children as old as 13 can become depressed or anxious after seeing upsetting events on TV. As your child gets older, watch his reactions and try to limit his exposure to life's horrors to a level he can handle. Often, when upsetting events are depicted on the TV news, children say they don't want to watch. These efforts should be respected, not belittled.

As to how to get your son on the airplane, we suggest that you tell him that while the plane crash was indeed upsetting to watch, that plane was very different than the one he will be flying on. You might also tell him the airlines will have learned from the crash so they can avoid the problem. Most importantly, assure him you are not worried. Tell him that perhaps when you get on board the pilot might be willing to reassure him in person. If none of this works and your son remains excessively fearful, it might be better to drive or take a train this time, if possible, and let the images of the plane crash fade from his mind for a time.

Standing up for herself

Q Help! When my daughter was an infant to her tot years, it seemed as if all the kids were picking on her. Now that she is five and able to give them some of their own medicine, her mom (me) is always saying that's not nice. My question is how can I break this habit of mine and let her stand up for herself? I know I should, but I find myself saying the same thing over and over or trying to explain what the meaning is behind the other kids' actions, and that makes things worse.

A If you find yourself saying that your daughter's behavior is "not nice" or talking about the other child's feelings when your daughter is defending herself, one problem is that you are using a model of relating that is too adult for your daughter's age.

It is always healthy to stand up for oneself and resist abuse, but at five, that self-defense may involve pushing and shoving as well as strong words. Five-year-olds are way too young to have to worry about the feelings of the person bullying them. So you are right to worry that it will harm your daughter's emotional development to tell her that it is "not nice" to protect or defend herself.

If you realize that you are finding it difficult to be positive when your daughter stands up for herself, it may be that you are reliving some similar situation from your childhood in which you were made to feel that it was wrong to defend yourself. If despite all your good intentions and your knowledge of how you should respond, you can't stop yourself from being negative, it might help to speak with a professional who can help you feel more comfortable with your daughter's healthy wish to protect herself.

How can I cope when my son wants mom, not me?

Q I am a very involved and devoted dad, but lately I have been feeling frustrated and alienated from my five-year-old son. Whenever he wants something, he asks his mom for it, even if she is in another room and I am sitting right next to him.

He only wants her to put him to bed and to play with him. If I offer to play ball or build something, he says no, he wants his mother. I have always tried to spend time with my son and I love him very much but this behavior makes no sense and is very hurtful to me. I also worry that my son is becoming a "mama's boy." I have told my wife she should insist that my son do some things with me. She says that wouldn't be good for him, that he should be with the parent he wants to be with. This disagreement is causing friction in our marriage. Can you advise please?

A Unfortunately, many parents suffer the kind of hurt feelings you are experiencing because they don't realize that it is entirely normal for children to go through a phase (which we call the romantic phase) in which they prefer the opposite-sex parent.

Between the ages of three and about six, children realize their parents have a special kind of relationship and they want the admiration and special attention they see the opposite-sex parent giving the same-sex parent. When that attention is not forthcoming, they conclude that the problem is the same-sex parent and become angry at that parent for being in the way. Children don't realize that the special attention the opposite-sex parent gives the same-sex parent is not going to be available to them regardless of the presence or absence of the same-sex parent.

So your son is acting normally. He is rejecting you only because he thinks you are interfering with his wish to have the romantic attention he wants but can't get from his mom. Underneath, he still adores you and is secretly hoping you won't be angry at him for trying to take your place.

If you can remain positive and accepting when he wants to be with his mother rather than with you, you will show your son that your love is not conditional.

In other words, if you remain understanding and loving, your son will eventually choose the pleasure of feeling close to both his mom and you over the impossible task of winning his mom away from you. The tensions in your marriage will ease as well.

Discouraging a child from following bad examples

Q My six-year-old son is in first grade and he has looked up to an older classmate since kindergarten. This other child is pleasant but very active and gets into trouble constantly. The problem is that my son is following this other student and is misbehaving and being disruptive in the classroom. My husband and I have taken away TV time, and we talk to him constantly about his behavior, the importance of not following other students, and of thinking for himself. However, this behavior continues and his academic performance is starting to suffer as a result. The school only has one first grade class, so I don't have the option of putting him in another room. We were thinking about transferring him to another school although I realize that the problem is within my son. It seems like talking to him isn't effective, and I feel helpless watching this take place. Please give us some advice on how to deal with this situation.

A While it appears to you that your son is under the spell of the older boy, in reality he chose him for a friend out of all the other children in his class, and he continues to want to be with him and to be like him. The implication is that even if you transfer him to another school, he may once again make an alliance with the most disruptive boy in his class.

The real problem is that your son finds the experience of disrupting his class and getting in trouble somehow attractive. Punishing him or lecturing him will only make things worse, because he will assume that your negative responses, though unpleasant, are "good" because they come from you. He may react by becoming even more driven to get the same kind of negative responses from teachers and other important adults.

We recommend that for the next six months or so, you go out of your way to relate to your son in a warm and positive way. Your goal is to show him that relationships with adults do not have to be filled with conflict and negativity. Look for times when you can compliment him. Try to think of activities he particularly likes doing with you (throwing a ball, going for walks, going to children's museums). Avoid scolding, withholding privileges, time-outs, or other forms of discipline as they will only prompt him to provoke similar negative responses from teachers. If he does something he is not supposed to do, such as picking a fight with a sibling, remain friendly as you steer him in another direction. You might say, "I don't think your brother liked what you did. If you're feeling annoyed with him right now, why don't you come with me and we'll find something fun to do?" Over time, your son probably will respond to the genuine pleasure of experiencing a thoroughly enjoyable relationship with you. His classroom behavior will change as he increasingly seeks similarly pleasant responses from his teachers. We would expect that he would also lose interest in the older boy because he will no longer find it so appealing to get in trouble and be criticized for his behavior.

If, on the other hand, you find that many months have gone by and your son is still driven to disrupt the class, in addition to maintaining a consistently positive relationship with him, you should also provide him with some form of professional counseling. A warm and committed counselor can help him to become more attracted to positive relationships and less interested in conflict and negativity.

Emotional Preschooler

Q I have very little tolerance and patience with my four-year-old son who cries in an instant when he's frustrated or doesn't get his way. While I know that he is an emotional child, his behavior annoys me. I am open to any suggestions on how to deal with this situation and to help him get a handle on his emotions.

A Like many parents, without realizing it, you are expecting too much of your child. One result is that there is tension and conflict in your relationship at times when there could be closeness and affection. While we all hope that our children will grow up to handle frustration well, the irony is that it is counterproductive to expect them to cope well with frustration as children. Parents often are not aware of the ways in which children's minds are very different from the minds of adults.

Every young child's sense of inner well-being is to a large extent dependent on getting what he wants when he wants it. This is a normal phase that will be gradually outgrown if parents understand this vulnerability and comfort their child when the inevitable meltdown occurs. When your son was younger, you may not have understood that it was normal for his self-esteem to crumble when he couldn't have what he wanted.

It is likely that the reason your son is so fragile now is not that he is "emotional," but that when he is frustrated, he has the double loss of feeling upset and also of knowing that you will be annoyed at him for coming unglued. We emphasize that when he cries, he is genuinely unhappy, and not willful, manipulative or deceptive.

The way to help him now is to respond to his tears and complaints by telling him that you know how badly he is feeling and that you want to help. Try to hold him; if he won't allow that, do stay with him in a comforting manner. Over time, the realization that he can count on you to remain positive and caring when things go wrong will make the experience of not getting what he wants seem less devastating. By understanding and responding to your son's true needs, you will replace the current moments of conflict and unhappiness with a loving closeness you can both enjoy.

Can 3-year-olds really learn how to share?

Q Could you revisit the issue of selfishness in children? I understand that you think 2-year-olds are too young to be made to share, but what about 3-year-olds? My son is 3 ½. While he has gotten better about sharing his toys and is less likely to grab from other children at the playground, he has his bad days. On a bad day he will melt down at the thought of having to let a friend play with one of his toys, and he is a holy terror when another child has a toy he wants. We think he is old enough now to share and not grab and we insist that he behave. The problem is that when we make him give up a toy, be becomes enraged and says he hates us. We isolate him for the rude language, but it makes us feel bad. We are trying to do the right thing, but it doesn't seem to be working. Are we expecting too much, or are we not being firm enough?

A Three-year-olds certainly look and act more mature than 2-year-olds. On a good day they can love their friends and want to share. But maturation never proceeds in a straight line. If children have a cold, things are tense at home, a best friend said something mean or they didn't get a turn painting at preschool, they can revert back to comforting themselves by going for the thing they want without regard for others.

It is so important to allow kids the space to regress on occasion without shaming or punishing them. Power struggles about sharing will just prolong the day when your child will be consistently reasonable about playing with others. If your 3-year-old has trouble sharing on a given day, respond with the understanding you gave him when he was 2. This way, when he does share, he will do it for the right reason—that it is a choice he is making to value friendships more than things.

What do we do about backseat squabbles?

 We are about to take our annual summer car trip with our two children, a four-year-old girl and a six-year-old boy, and we badly need advice.

Last summer we drove to a lake in Northern Wisconsin, and what was supposed to be a pleasant family vacation turned into the trip from hell. The kids fought from the moment we left until we arrived. They argued about everything from who was taking up more room on the seat to who got more of the food. On the few occasions they actually tried to play a game together, they ended up by accusing each other of cheating. The most pleasant part of the trip was when they actually stopped speaking to each other for a while.

I'm not sure why we're trying this again. Maybe we're just gluttons for punishment. Is there a way to make the drive less painful for them and us? We have the same sorts of problems going to school every morning, but the ride is shorter so it's not so bad.

A Yours is not an uncommon problem. Even siblings who normally get along well can wage World War III in the back seat during a long trip. This is truly a case in which an ounce of prevention is not only worth a pound of cure but will save your sanity and make you like family vacations again. Here are some suggestions:

- Bring more food than four children could possibly eat.
- Break up the ride so you never go more than two hours without a two-minute break.
- During the break, get the kids running, jumping or playing ball.
- For the in-car part of the trip, put together a goody bag that includes mazes, new books, finger puppets, and more. There are also the classic car games such as looking out the window and seeing how many cows, red cars, etc., each person can see. When all of the above lose their appeal, play a book on tape that

they would both enjoy.

Mainly remember that fighting is usually a response to boredom. You probably have ideas of your own to keep the kids occupied.

If the trip out is nightmarish in spite of your best efforts, as a last resort on the way home, have one parent drive and the other sit in the middle of the back seat. Alternatively, if you can handle it, leave at 1:00 a.m. and drive at night.

How do we make family road trips bearable?

Q We are about to take a driving vacation to see relatives in Oregon, and our children, a boy, 3; a girl, 5; made our last trip a living hell. They fought every day from the time we started to the time we stopped. Sometimes they confine their hostility to words, which is unpleasant enough because they call each other horrible names and make each other cry. But when we tell them not to talk, they reach over and pinch or hit each other and there is more screaming. We tell them we are going to go back home, but they know we don't mean it. We tell them we are going to take away privileges such as using the motel pool and that sometimes works for a bit—but not for long. They squabble at home quite a bit, but nothing like what happens in the car. How can we make the trip bearable for them AND us?

A Long drives with children require advance planning to make them pleasant. Have some new toys or activities to fill some of the time. Parcel those out over the drive rather than all at once. Travel stores tend to have good games and toys for the car. If you have a computer or DVD player, allowing the kids to see a movie once a day usually results in two hours of peace. You can also try audio books or song tapes.

However, if a 3- and 5-year-old are to spend long hours in a car together, it may become necessary for you or your husband to sit between them in the back seat for a while. Use the time sitting between them to read a book, sing songs or find things in the passing landscape (black cows, red cars, etc). The goal is not to punish them but to offer constructive help.

Also, plan the trip so you can stop every hour or two and let them out for a romp. The principle is not to be upset or angry with them for their age-appropriate inability to tolerate long periods in the car.

Spanking stops behavior, but can it hurt the child?

Q My wife is convinced there is nothing wrong with giving our four-year-old a swat on the bottom when he persists in doing something he has been told not to do. She would never hit him with a belt or hit him in the face, but she is convinced that a slap on the bottom is the only response that works.

For example, yesterday he wanted a cookie. My wife said he couldn't have it before dinner. He ignored her and climbed on the counter and started trying to reach the cookie jar in the cabinet. She told him to stop or she would spank him. He didn't stop, so she slapped him on the bottom. He started to cry but he did stop trying to reach the cookies.

Spanking does seem to work, but I worry about the long-term effects on my son.

A You are right to worry. Hitting people who don't do what we want is the worst lesson we can teach our children. Parents can get so caught up in controlling behavior in the short term that they don't think about the long-term consequences of their methods. Spanking teaches children that hurting others is an acceptable solution to differences of opinion. For this reason, swats on the bottom are never harmless or inconsequential.

We recommend loving regulation to manage your son. Loving regulation separates the punitive component from the regulatory component of managing children's behavior. For example, if your son is attracted to cookies before dinner, you can probably avoid the problem altogether by having a locked cabinet or putting them in a place he won't think to look. Preventing conflict is a crucial strategy in parenting young children.

If the cookies are within reach and he is determined to have one, rather than expecting him to control his desires, move the cookies where he can't reach them, pick him up and hug him when he cries, and offer him a healthy snack to tide him over. You will have achieved your goal of preventing him from spoiling his appetite with sweets, while at the same time showing him you can disagree with his behavior and still love and care for him. Unlike spanking, loving regulation provides children with a model of peaceful yet effective ways to solve relationship differences.

❤

Testing for a speech disorder

Q As a stay-at-home mother, spending all my time with my child, I have always been able to understand my four-year-old's speech. However, a couple of my family members have frequently asked me to interpret what my child is saying, and now my child's preschool teacher recommends I have him tested for speech. How does a parent such as myself—a stay-at-home mother who is constantly in contact with her child—know when to question whether her child may or may not have a speech disorder?

A Since you can understand your son's speech, your doubts about whether he needs an evaluation are very understandable. A good rule of thumb is that if his preschool teacher thinks your son's speech needs evaluating, you should follow her advice. The teacher sees so many children your son's age that she is in a position to know whether his indistinct speech is in the range of a normal developmental variation or is part of a pattern that calls for evaluation.

Evaluation will make it possible to rule out any physical problems your son may have with sound production or sound reception. Do choose an evaluator who is positive and kind, so that the process of evaluation will not be upsetting to your son.

Most important is to protect your son from feeling something is seriously wrong. You could just say matter-of-factly that you know it must be frustrating when people have trouble understanding him and that you want to help him so that the important things he has to say will be understood all of the time.

How do I teach my son not to take things from pre-school?

Q Help! Lately my four-year-old has been bringing small toys home from preschool. I have been finding Legos and plastic animals in his backpack or his pants pocket. When I ask him about it, he says he found them. I know that he is taking them from school without asking, but he won't admit it.

Why is he stealing, and how do I best help him understand that he can't take things that don't belong to him?

A Your son is way too young for his actions to be thought of as "stealing." His taking things is an emotional issue and not a moral issue.

Your son is feeling upset about something, and he is trying to make himself feel better by bringing toys home. If you cast his behavior in terms of right and wrong, you will feel upset with and disappointed in your son, which will be painful for both of you and harmful to him. The worse you make him feel, the greater will be his need to comfort himself by putting toys in his pockets. So the irony is that he will be more disposed to steal in the future if he is accused of stealing now.

Rather, try to understand why your son suddenly feels the need to take things. We would guess that like many young children, he likes his school and hates to see the school year end. He is bringing part of school home with him as a way of coping with the fact that the school year is nearly over. His behavior is an age-appropriate attempt to recognize and deal with an impending loss.

What you need to do is to get the problem into the open and show your son a better solution. Talk to him about how difficult it is to be leaving his classroom, his friends, and his teacher for the summer. Tell him you know that is why he is bringing toys home from school and that you understand that he hopes they will make him feel better. Add that while the toys have to go back, you will go with him to tell his teacher how he is feeling and to ask if there is something from the classroom that could come home for the summer. Perhaps he would be allowed to take the class hamster or a plant, or the teacher would decorate a card for him that he could hang in his room.

Most important, once you understand what is bothering your son and realize that his way of trying to soothe himself is not "wrong" but is actually appropriate for his age, you will be able to solve the problem in a way that allows both of you to maintain a close and loving relationship.

Should I insist that my four-year-old continue going to summer camp?

Q My four-year-old, who had a successful first year in preschool, was supposed to be in a summer camp doing sports, art, etc. He was really looking forward to it, so I was amazed when he came home after the first day and said he didn't want to go back.

I have been forcing him to go because I think it will be good for him and I'm sure he will like it if he gives it a chance, but he is actually becoming more, rather than less, resistant. I am afraid to give in and let him think he can dictate what he will and won't do. Please advise.

A The real issue is not whether you are going to allow your son to dictate to you; it's when to make a child do something he doesn't want to do.

The best principle for making this decision is only to insist when the behavior is necessary (for health, safety, family needs, etc.). It's never a good idea to make children do something just to establish that you are more powerful than they are and can order them around. In fact, teaching children that "might makes right" is a bad idea that boomerangs as children get older and stronger. Applying this principle to your son's summer vacation, think of it as a time when he has free time and should have relatively free choice. Even though your son was happily looking forward to summer camp, something about the reality of going to it has turned him off. Since he is unhappy about going, try to enroll him in a different program. Or if you are not working, perhaps he would be happiest staying home with you and going on outings to the beach, the park or the zoo. You will accomplish much by showing your son that whenever possible you will honor his preferences. He will know that you value his choices and as he grows up, he will copy you and learn to respect the choices of others. For now, the knowledge that you want to honor his wishes will help him to be more accepting at those times when you can't do as he wants.

How do I convince my son he should learn to swim?

Q We are planning a vacation in August and have rented a house on a lake. The problem is that our six-year-old son refuses to learn to swim, and I am very concerned about being so close to water when he wouldn't be able to cope if he fell in.

Also, there are rowboats and canoes available that we can't allow him to use if he can't swim. His two older siblings are good swimmers and like the water, but he becomes hysterical if we try to show him how to swim. We have tried every trick to get him to take swim classes, but he won't go.

This vacation is looking as though it will make everyone miserable. Do you have any suggestions?

A The important thing is to distinguish health and safety concerns from your irritation that your son doesn't want to swim. Pushing a child to engage in an activity that frightens him simply solidifies his resistance. In the past, children who didn't want to swim were actually thrown into the water, with the result that many of these children hated swimming for the rest of their lives and didn't trust adults much, either.

You need to make sure your son understands that you will not pressure him to learn to swim, but that because he is a non-swimmer, certain health and safety rules apply. For example, he can't go anywhere near the water without an adult, and he cannot go on a dock or wade into the water without wearing a lifejacket. Explain that he will be able to do some boating if an adult is along and he wears his life jacket. Most important, state and enforce these rules in a way that makes clear that they are not punishments but arise from your love and concern for him.

If he is around other children who enjoy the water and can paddle around in a life jacket without being pressured to swim, your son may well decide on his own that he is ready to become a swimmer.

Will teasing harm my preschooler?

Q What is your position about adults teasing children? We have a three-year-old girl and my husband teases her a lot. For example, he will tell her there is a bear behind her, or that she has a grease spot on her dress, or that she can't have the ice cream cone she had been promised. When she becomes upset, he says he is "just kidding." I can't see the humor in it, but he assures me that it's good for her to learn to take a joke and that kids will tease her all the time at school. What should I do?

A You should tell your husband that he has a badly distorted idea of children's emotional needs. Above all, your daughter looks to you to tell her the truth, to comfort her and to make her feel secure and loved. When your husband teases her, he causes her to doubt that she is safe and cared for. That insecurity will actually make her more vulnerable to other children's taunts.

Teasing is never good for young children. No matter what the age, teasing should be very benign. For example, it's OK to say when sitting down to dinner at a restaurant with your one-year-old, "I know you're going to order Brussels sprouts because they're your favorite food," but it would not be all right to say, "Let's ask for the diet menu for kids who need to lose weight."

When/how should I tell my twin 3-year-olds that I'm pregnant?

Q When and how should I tell my 3-year-old twins that I'm pregnant? Should we tell them what the sex is to help prepare them?

A In general, we recommend telling children that they are going to have a little sister or brother when the first trimester is over and the pregnancy is well-established. Children are amazingly tuned into their mothers, and if they are not told of the pregnancy by the second trimester, they can become quite upset by changes they perceive but cannot explain. Also, telling your children early will minimize their sense of displacement, because they will have 6 more months of being the undivided focus of all your caregiving attention. This principle is particularly important to twins, who have had to share you from the beginning.

The best way to tell your twins about the new arrival is briefly and simply. For example, you might say, "You're going to have a new brother (or sister). Right now he is growing inside Mommy, but he will be ready to come out some time next spring." By not overloading your children with facts, you leave them the space to absorb the startling revelation at their rate of speed and to ask questions when they are ready to hear more. There is no downside to telling the twins the sex of the new arrival, and it will help make the upcoming birth more real to them.

How should I handle a preschool biting incident?

Q My three-year-old is in a private preschool. Lately he has been complaining about a classmate who is biting other children. Yesterday he came home with bite marks on his arm. The skin wasn't broken, but there is a bruise that is clearly from a set of teeth.

I asked my son what the teacher did and he said he didn't tell her because he was afraid the biter would get angry and bite him again. He added that when children have complained, the teacher just tells the biter to stop biting-an intervention that clearly is not working.

In this day of HIV and other blood diseases, this behavior is especially frightening to me. Plus, I have noticed that my son has started talking about hurting and killing people, which he never did before.

What should I say to him and should I call the school?

A It is crucial that you make clear to your son that you do not expect him to cope with this problem by himself and that you will protect him from this aggressive behavior. Explain to him that biting another child is absolutely unacceptable and that you will talk to the teacher and find a way to protect him and all the other children in the class from the biter. Make an appointment with the teacher (include any other parents who are interested in joining you) and insist that the biting behavior be completely controlled — if necessary by isolating the biting child or sending him home. Explain that you are concerned about infections as well as about the psychological and physical harm the child is inflicting.

Clearly the biter needs psychological help, but until he gets it, it is the responsibility of the teacher to make sure his classmates' safety is assured.

If the teacher seems reluctant or unable to take appropriate action, ask that your child be moved to another classroom. Once your child feels safe again, he will most likely stop soothing himself with aggressive fantasies of hurting others.

Helping kids cope with rough peers

Q This summer, my six-year-old son—who is very physical but also very emotionally sensitive—was in a two-week day camp where a lot of boys behaved in ways that he had not been exposed to before. There was lots of teasing and physically aggressive play.

Every day he came home with a story about how his feelings were hurt. Some of the offenses were unintentional or even appropriate (e.g., someone else won a relay race) but some were mean-spirited and genuinely hurtful (e.g., kids teased him for having a "girl's backpack" and made fun of his name, and one even threatened him physically).

His usual response to these things was to tell a counselor, and they generally spoke to the other kids. But he was also coming home feeling sad and angry. How can I help him, at this young age, to develop more of a thick skin without encouraging him to be less sensitive? I hate to see him lose his sweetness and openness.

A This is a tough situation for any parent. You take care from the moment of his birth to give your child kindness and to make his life as pleasant as possible, and then he goes to camp and encounters other children who treat him badly and make him unhappy.

Although it's too late now, the first response would have been to ask your son if he wanted to continue with camp. Unlike school, camp is optional and only for recreation. It would have been good to give your son the opportunity to decide if camp was making him more unhappy than happy.

Your objective is not to help your son develop a "thick skin," that is, to become impervious to rude or cruel behavior by others, but rather to help him find a variety of constructive ways to respond. The best and most important response is the one he already turned to, which is to tell you that his feelings are hurt. Just hearing you say that what the other children said or did was mean and that he deserves to be treated better is the best medicine there is. Do encourage him to continue to tell you when he has been made to feel bad. Don't make him feel embarrassed or ashamed because his feelings are easily hurt, because then he will find it difficult to confide in you.

There are numerous other ways your son could cope with children who are picking on him. Telling the counselor is one he already thought of. Ignoring the teasers is another. If you help your son to understand that children only pick on other children because they themselves are unhappy inside and feel that "misery loves company," he will see that if he ignores the teasers, they will be robbed of the gratification they seek and may focus their mean remarks elsewhere.

Helping children cope with tragedy

In the wake of the tragic events of September 11th, parents have repeatedly asked us how best to help their children cope when they are exposed to a horrifying reality. We would like to devote this column to a discussion of how to respond to your children so as to minimize the possibility that they will be traumatized by what they have heard or seen of the terrible events that have rocked the country.

For children under age fourteen, try to minimize their exposure to radio and television coverage of the disaster. You would not want your children to watch violent movies, and realistic descriptions of planes crashing into buildings and bodies falling out of the sky are more frightening than any movie.

Television images will be especially difficult for children to get out of their minds. Very young children may be especially frightened because their immaturity may cause them to believe that the scenes pictured are right in their neighborhood and are still happening.

Do not overwhelm children with information. When giving children bad news, it is always best to give the bare facts followed by reassurance that the worst is over. Then follow their lead about how much more they are ready to hear. When a young child who has heard that something bad has happened asks you what is wrong, you might say something like, "Some planes hit buildings and the buildings caught on fire." You might tell an older child, "Some very bad people stole airplanes and crashed them into buildings."

Ask children if they have any questions, but if they are not ready to talk, let them come to grips with the news on their own timetable. One nine-year-old we know reacted to the grim news by trying to solve the problem. He responded cheerfully, "They should just cover the buildings with steel so airplanes wouldn't go through." He wasn't interested in further discussion and his parents didn't pressure him.

That night when they were putting their son to bed, his parents asked, "How are you feeling?" He burst into tears and said, "I want to move from our apartment to a small house that airplanes can't get to." At that point, he was ready to ask many questions about why people would behave that way and what had happened to the people in the buildings. He was also relieved to be reassured that there were no more airplanes with bad people in the sky.

Let your children know you are affected by the tragedy, while at the same time you show them you are optimistic about the future. Children often feel there is something wrong with being upset or expressing upset feelings; this is an opportunity to tell them that you and other adults feel troubled, too, because these events are really disturbing.

At the same time, it is important not to share with children pessimistic thoughts such as, "The world will never be the same," but to offer them optimism. "This is over now, and our government will catch the bad people who did this." Your children have such faith in your opinion, they will take your pessimism to mean that the whole world has become a terrible place, but they will also be very reassured by your optimism that things can get back to normal.

Try not to use tragedy as an object lesson about the world. This is not the moment to tell children, "See, there are bad people in the world; this is why you shouldn't talk to strangers." Children need to be reassured that they and the people they love are safe, and not to have their fears heightened.

Don't interfere with your children's coping mechanisms. Children have many ways of protecting themselves from the full awfulness of the tragedy. For example, they may make light of what has happened. One mother was horrified when her young child saw a photo of a plane hitting one of the Trade Towers and said, "That's cool." She immediately told him that this was "for real" and that "lots of mommies and daddies died in the fire." At the point the child burst into tears and became hysterical.

Puncturing children's denial of the awfulness of events may flood them with painful emotions they are not ready to handle. Take your cue from your children, and wait for a time when they are ready to deal with their feelings more directly.

Give your children some slack. Children often show their upset feelings by becoming irritable, fearful, having trouble sleeping, fighting with siblings, or bursting into tears at the slightest frustration. These behaviors may continue for weeks. It's important to keep this in mind, so that instead of saying, "What on earth has gotten into you," when your eight-year-old bursts into tears because his jacket zipper is stuck, you can say, "I can see you are really upset. Maybe you're still thinking about the terrible things that happened. I still feel badly about them, too."

Don't be surprised if your children become fearful about everyday activities. Children may react to hearing about tragedy by worrying about going to school or about seeing their parents go to work. If you encourage them to talk about why they are afraid to go to school or to have you go to work, you may get some clue to what they are really worried about. One seven-year-old who became hysterical when his father left for work insisted that his office building was going to fall down. A five-year-old who couldn't sleep finally got under his bed, "so the ceiling can't land on me." These expressions of fears are opportunities to reassure your child that it is normal to feel upset and worried when something so terrible has happened, but that everything is OK now.

Make yourself more available than usual. One of the most helpful things you can do to help your children cope with the news of a disaster is to spend as much time as possible with them. Children always feel safest in their parents' presence. And the more comfortable and secure they feel, the better able they will be to bring up concerns and questions.

Helping children cope with tragedies and disasters
- Minimize their exposure to radio and television coverage of the disaster.
- Do not overwhelm them with information.
- Follow their lead about how much more they are ready to hear.
- Let them come to grips with the news on their own timetable.
- Let them know you are affected by the tragedy, while at the same time showing you are optimistic about the future.
- Try not to use tragedy as an object lesson about the world.
- Don't interfere with your children's coping mechanisms.
- Give your children some slack.
- If your children become fearful about everyday activities, encourage them to talk about why they are afraid.
- Reassure your children that it is normal to feel upset and worried when something so terrible has happened, but that everything is OK now.
- Make yourself more available than usual.

Difficulty saying "good-bye"

Q Our five-year-old daughter seems to have difficulty with departures. When it is time to leave a social situation such as a visit at Grandma's house or a playmate's house, she invariably fusses loudly and resists putting on her coat and shoes to leave.

We try to give her advance notice that we will be going home soon, but are still met with resistance. We encourage her to say a nice good-bye and thank you to our hosts, but she often ends up leaving with an unhappy pout on her face. What are your thoughts on this situation and do you have any suggestions how we can help our daughter learn to leave gracefully?

A Your daughter will learn to leave gracefully, but not until she is older. At five, transitions are still hard for her, especially when she has to give up an enjoyable experience, such as visiting Grandma or a playmate. Older children have a more sophisticated understanding of time. They know how long a two-hour visit is, and accept that when the time is up, they will have to go. Five-year-olds often feel that endings are arbitrary and negotiable, especially when they are having fun. This is the reason that leaving gracefully is not always in their power.

Although at this age your daughter is unlikely to leave a place she likes smiling and saying her "thank you," there are strategies you can use to ease your daughter's transitions. Most important, show her that you understand how difficult it is for her to give up an activity she is enjoying. You might say something like, "We know you love being with Grandma and it's really hard to go. Let's make a date for another visit. How about next Saturday?"

When you first arrive, tell your daughter what time the visit will end by showing her where the hands will be on the kitchen clock. When she sees that the clock hands have reached the ending time, leaving will seem less arbitrary to her. Give her a few minutes to get used to the idea of going. Try to have some future fun in mind to help her exit. For example, tell her that you brought her dog and he's waiting in the car, or that when you get home you will make play dough for her.

Finally, don't expect a five-year-old struggling with her dismay at having to leave to be able to say a polite and grown-up good-bye. We suggest that you step in and be gracious for her. You might say, "You can see how much my daughter loved being with you; she hates to leave. Thank you so much for having her." When your daughter is old enough to feel comfortable with transitions, she will also be ready to make the gracious good-byes that elude her now.

Is a five-year-old able to cope with the stress of "reel" life?

Q We have a five-year-old who wants us to take her to movies she says friends are talking about. If the movies contain more violence and death than we think she is ready for, we tell her she can go when she is older.

But what do we say about movies that are in a gray area? An example is "Finding Nemo," which starts with the mother being eaten. Then little Nemo is taken from his father and shut up in an aquarium.

She really wants to see the movie, but we don't know whether it will be a positive experience for her.

A It has always seemed unfortunate to us that so many books and movies intended for children use the death of one or both parents as a plot device. We agree that, given her age, it is difficult to say whether your daughter will find the movie more enjoyable than upsetting.

Probably the best thing to do in this case is describe the plot to her and ask her how she feels about going to a movie in which the mother is eaten and the baby fish gets taken away from his father. (You can add that the baby fish does get back to his father in the end.) Young children are unlike adults in that knowing the ending doesn't spoil the fun. Make clear to your daughter that if she doesn't feel she wants to see a movie with that plot, she can watch it on video when she is older.

If your daughter does decide to see the movie, at least she will not be taken by surprise by the sad parts. If she enjoys the show and does not subsequently have nightmares or become more anxious than usual, she is old enough to make decisions about what she will enjoy if you inform her ahead of time about potentially disturbing parts of the story. However, if she decides she wants to see the movie but then becomes upset in the theater or in the days following, then for the time being she needs to be sheltered from exposure to sad or scary stories.

My four-year-old will not stop whining—what can we do?

Q Could you please revisit the issue of whining? Our four-year-old is driving us insane. Whenever he wants something, he kicks into whining mode. Even when his request is otherwise reasonable, we don't want to give it to him when he whines because we feel it rewards this behavior. But when he doesn't get what he wants, he whines even more. My neighbor told me she read a book that advised her to tell her whining child, "I don't want to be with you when you act like that—I don't listen to your whining voice but I listen to your nice voice." When she says that, her child usually stops whining. What do you think of that approach—it seems harsh to me—and do you have other suggestions?

A You are correct that your neighbor's approach to whining is too harsh. Appealing as it can sometimes be in the short run to browbeat children into behaving as you wish, in the long run, you teach children the unintended lessons that might makes right and that they can't count on your good will when they feel upset or out of sorts. Children who absorb these lessons often grow into adults who run roughshod over other's feelings and struggle to be compassionate with themselves and others.

When your child whines, it is much better to ignore the whining and respond as though he were speaking in a normal voice. If he says he needs something "right now" and what he wants is something he can have, say, "Sure, no problem," and let him have it. If he can't have what he desires and whines about it, don't focus on the whining. Show him that you know it's hard when he can't have what he wants. When whining simply ceases to become an issue for you and when your son knows that you want him to have his heart's desire whenever possible and you are sympathetic when he has a disappointment, clinical experience tells us that your son will stop whining. Most important, he will stop because whining has lost its appeal and not because he has been threatened or is worried about keeping your love and good will.

Supernanny's quick fixes fail in the long run

Q Could you please comment on the TV show "Supernanny"? The nanny seems to get good results, but she seems kind of hard on the children. My kids (two boys, 2 and 6; and a girl, 4) tend to run around and make a lot of noise when playing. They usually aren't crying or fighting, but things get pretty rowdy and it's hard to have an adult conversation. When my mother visited, she said the kids were "out of control" and that I should watch "Supernanny" and take her advice to heart. I felt hurt and don't know what to do. Honestly, I like to see the kids having fun, but I don't want to let them run wild in a way that will be bad for them in the long run. Suggestions?

A It sounds as though your children are enjoying their lives. Enthusiasm is a good thing, not a sign of being "out of control." When kids are truly out of control, the Supernanny approach is appealing in that, as if by magic, she drops in, assesses the situation, applies a quick fix and leaves with everything in good order.

First, remember that this is television. There is a lot of footage we do not see and there is no long-term follow-up. Second, there are harmful long-term consequences to short-term fixes that use punishments and criticism. Supernanny's assumption is that children will manipulate and take advantage of parents. In reality, children are born wanting loving relationships with their parents.

When kids get out of control, it is usually because they are managed either with too much harshness or too little loving regulation. The answer is not to use adult power harshly, which alienates them. For example, when Supernanny forces kids to apologize to parents, children say they are sorry even though they are resentful. What these kids are actually learning is to hide their true feelings behind the pretense of social correctness—not a good lesson for a happy life.

Parents must learn how to manage their kids' behavior in a positive way that incorporates reasonable expectations for different ages and stages. Unfortunately, good parenting advice is probably not dramatic enough for TV, so parents will continue to be misled by programs like this one.

Index